D1505232

A CLASSIC RETELLING

Stories and Poems of

EDGAR ALLAN POE

nextext

Printed in the United States of America
ISBN 0-618-08598-X

2 3 4 5 6 7 8 9 — QKT — 06 05 04 03 02

Picture Acknowledgements

Page 9 © North Wind Picture Archives

Page 11 © The Granger Collection

Page 14 © Mary Evans Picture Library/Harry Clarke

Page 17 © Mary Evans Picture Library/Arthur Rackham

Page 19 © Mary Evans Picture Library/Arthur Rackham

Page 20 © North Wind Picture Archives

Page 21 © Mary Evans Picture Library

Page 23 © Mary Evans Picture Library

Table of Contents

SHORT STORIES

Like many of Poe's stories, "The Pit and the
Pendulum" (1842) is told through the eyes
of one person, the narrator. In this case,
the narrator has been sentenced to die by the
Spanish Inquisition.

This story, published in 1842, is set in the Middle
Ages. As a result of the Red Death, a deadly
disease that scholars now believe was originally
spread by rats, more than half of Prince
Prospero's kingdom lies dead. Rather than try to
help, however, the prince decides to shut himself
in with a thousand friends and live in luxury.

*"The Raven" (1845) gave Poe his first major
success as a writer. Poe's purpose for writing this
poem was simple. He wanted to show his
readers a mind filled with "fantastic terrors."*

*Vocabulary words appear in boldface type and are
footnoted. Specialized or technical words and phrases
appear in lightface type and are footnoted.*

Background

Edgar Allan Poe
(1809–1849)

Hundreds of books, articles, and Internet pages have been written about Edgar Allan Poe. Even so, no one is really sure who Poe was. Many people say that he was as crazy as the characters he wrote about. Others say that Poe was a driven man with a simple wish. He wanted to write and to make a living by his writing. Even though Poe lived a miserable life, he wrote some of the most interesting and original literature ever created.

Edgar Poe was born in Boston in 1809. His English mother and Irish father were traveling actors. When Edgar was two years old, his father, whose career was destroyed by alcohol, left the family. Poe's mother died soon after in 1811.

Young Edgar was sent to live with John Allan, a wealthy Virginia merchant, and his wife. The Allans moved to England when Edgar was six. Poe went to school there. After five years, the Allans returned to the United States in 1820. Although the Allans were kind, Poe quarreled a great deal with John Allan.

When Poe was seventeen, he was accepted at the University of Virginia. Although he did well at school, he had to leave the university at the end of his first year because Allan refused to pay for Poe's gambling debts.

Poe moved to Boston, where he worked at many different jobs. At each new job, he did well for a while and then lost his job because of quarrels or his own bad habits.

In 1827, Poe published a small book of poems called *Tamerlane and Other Poems*. It was ignored by almost everyone. In 1832, he moved to Baltimore, and in 1835, he secretly married his cousin, Virginia, who was thirteen-years-old at the time. A year later, they had a public wedding.

Edgar Allan Poe

No one is sure if Poe had mental problems, but he did have trouble with alcoholism. Poe drank heavily through his twenties and into his thirties. He was often drunk on the job, which led to more firings.

Poe continued to publish poems and short stories, including, in 1841, "The Murders in the Rue Morgue." This story is thought to be the first modern detective story. But still no one paid any attention to his work. At this point the Poes, who . had never had enough money, became desperately poor. Worse yet, in 1842, Virginia broke a blood vessel in her throat while singing. She recovered, but afterwards she fell ill again and again.

Over the next few years, Poe tried one job after another. He wrote a little and drank a great deal. At one point, he explained that his drinking was not for pleasure but "a desperate attempt to escape bad memories . . . loneliness . . . and some strange impending doom."

In 1845, however, Poe's luck seemed to be turning. He wrote and published his poem "The Raven," which was an instant success. Suddenly, everyone wanted to meet the brilliant "new" author. Poe began to lecture about writing and published a new collection of short stories. Almost overnight, Poe's wish had come true. He was recognized as a major figure in New York City's literary circles. Yet in 1847, his beloved Virginia, who was still in her early twenties, died. Two years later, Poe himself was dead.

Most of his biographers say that Poe died of alcoholism. Some stories say that he died in a gutter. In 1996, however, a cardiologist named Dr. R. Michael Benitez reviewed Poe's autopsy and medical records. He concluded that Poe died in a hospital from rabies—after four days of screaming and hallucinating. If this is true, Poe's final days were like those of the characters he wrote about— mad and haunted.

Timeline

1809—Edgar Poe is born in Boston, Massachusetts.

1811—Young Edgar goes to live with the Allans.

1815–1820—The Allans take Edgar to live and be educated in England.

1826—Poe enrolls in the University of Virginia, but leaves after his freshman year.

1827—Using his own money, Poe publishes *Tamerlane and Other Poems*.

1835—Poe secretly marries his cousin, thirteen-year-old Virginia Clem.

1841—Poe's "The Murders in the Rue Morgue" is published.

1842—Virginia breaks a blood vessel in her throat, and her health becomes worse.

1845—"The Raven" is published. Critics call it "brilliant." Poe becomes famous almost overnight.

1847—Virginia Poe dies.

1849—Poe dies at age 40.

Poe's Short Stories

Edgar Allan Poe always thought of himself as a poet, but he is remembered most for his short stories. He had some very strong ideas about what a short story should be. First and foremost, he believed that a short story should be *short*—a person should be able to read it in one sitting. Poe also believed that a story should take a reader into a completely different world. Because of this, he wrote about things that were unusual. He never wrote a story about an everyday experience or a person you might meet on a street corner.

Settings

All of Poe's stories are set in some unknown place that readers can't recognize. Poe did this because he wanted readers to pay attention to the overall atmosphere of the setting. He wanted readers to feel the cold mist surrounding Roderick Usher's house in "The Fall of the House of Usher" and the dampness of Montresor's vault in "The Cask of Amontillado." He didn't want readers to watch for places they had been or scenes they had read about before. Poe said that any reader who could recognize a part of the setting as being familiar would be unable to think about the atmosphere and the beauty of the story.

The fate of Fortunato in "The Cask of Amontillado."

For the same reason, Poe was always vague about time in his stories. He never named a specific year in a story. Poe knew that if the time and place were a mystery, readers would not bother to look for people, places, or even objects that they knew. Instead, they would focus on the action and the writer's art.

Subjects

Like many writers of his day, Poe loved to write about the strange or supernatural. He felt very strongly that common or everyday subjects had no place in art. So he wrote about frightening experiences, bodies that returned from the dead, madness, and terrible events that no one had imagined before. Poe hated literature that dealt with everyday things, and he was never afraid to tell people that. For this reason, he made quite a few enemies in the literary circles of his day. As a book reviewer, Poe wrote many reviews that were famous for their sarcasm, wit, and put-downs.

Poe also enjoyed writing about mental illness. Many of his characters, such as Roderick Usher, Montresor in "The Cask of Amontillado," and the narrator of "The Tell-Tale Heart" are insane. Most of his characters who are not insane are guided more by their emotions than by their intelligence. Poe believed that people's emotions were far more interesting than their minds. This is why even his "normal" characters, such as Dupin in "The Murders in the Rue Morgue" and "The Purloined Letter," spend more time thinking about the "feel" of a place rather than how it looks or sounds.

Characters

Poe said that the characters of a story were not nearly as important as the setting and the subject matter. In many of his stories, including "The Pit and the Pendulum" and "The Tell-Tale Heart," his narrators are not named. Poe thought that the characters' actions and emotions showed who they were. He told readers to watch a character's behavior and not bother with such questions as "Who is this person?" and "What's his name?"

"I placed my chair over the spot where I had hidden the dead body!"
said the narrator in "The Tell-Tale Heart."

Poe and the Gothic Story

The Gothic period in American literature took place during the late-eighteenth and early-nineteenth centuries. Edgar Allan Poe is perhaps the most famous of America's Gothic writers. Others who wrote in the Gothic tradition include Mary Wollstonecraft Shelley (*Frankenstein*, 1818) and Bram Stoker (*Dracula*, 1898). Books by modern authors such as Anne Rice and Stephen King also have Gothic elements.

Gothic stories are known for their medieval or remote settings, their murky atmospheres of horror and gloom, and their violent, disturbing plots. Gothic stories involve:

• deserted houses, haunted mansions, or gloomy castles;

• ghosts, dead bodies, and the "undead" (dead bodies that have come back to life);

• highly emotional characters, many of whom are on the edge of total insanity;

• some form of communication between the living and the dead.

Poe's short story "The Fall of the House of Usher," which contains all four of the above elements, is thought to be one of the finest Gothic stories ever written.

What frightened the narrator of "The Fall of the House of Usher" when he saw this house?

Poe and Detective Fiction

Edgar Allan Poe is known as the father of the modern detective story. Many detective methods common today are used in "The Purloined Letter" and "The Murders in the Rue Morgue." These stories introduce tracking a suspect using deduction and imagining yourself in the mind of the criminal, which are used all the time in detective stories today. When these stories were published, however, no fictional detective had ever used these techniques.

In his detective fiction, Poe also introduced the idea of a crime being committed in a "closed room," with no visible means for escape. In "The Murders in the Rue Morgue," for example, Poe used the "closed room" to make his story more exciting. Readers kept reading to find out how the criminal (or the narrator) would find a way out of the room. Mystery writers such as Sir Arthur Conan Doyle (who wrote the Sherlock Holmes stories) and Agatha Christie used many of Poe's ideas in their own detective fiction.

Will the sharp pendulum kill him? Read "The Pit and the Pendulum."

Poe's Poetry

Poe wrote that poetry should be beautiful and sad at the same time. Truly beautiful things, he said, are so lovely that they hurt. This is why the tone of his poems is almost always sad.

> For the moon never beams without bringing me dreams
> Of the beautiful Annabel Lee;
> And the stars never rise but I see the bright eyes
> Of the beautiful Annabel Lee;
> And so, all the night-tide, I lie down by the side
> Of my darling, my darling, my life and my bride
> In her sepulchre there by the sea —
> In her tomb by the side of the sea.

A page of Poe's handwriting from an early version of "Annabel Lee."

A favorite subject of Poe's poetry was the death of a beautiful young woman. This may well have been because his own beloved wife, Virginia, was ill for several years and died when she was in her early twenties. In "Annabel Lee" and "To Helen," the speaker grieves deeply over the death of a young woman. Poe once said about these poems, "The death, then, of a beautiful woman is, unquestionably, the most poetical topic in the world."

Poe also believed that a poem should be short. He hated poems that went on for pages and pages. In his lectures, he would tell audiences that a poem longer than 110 lines should be ignored—unless it is broken up into smaller chunks. Interestingly, his most famous poem, "The Raven," came close to flunking his own test. It is 108 lines long.

A CLASSIC RETELLING

Stories and Poems of

EDGAR ALLAN POE

The Pit and the Pendulum

Like many of Poe's stories, "The Pit and the Pendulum"
(1842) is told through the eyes of one person, the
narrator. In this case, the narrator has been sentenced
to die by the Spanish Inquisition.

I was sick—sick to death of the pain and suffering.
I had been sick ever since they brought me into the
Inquisition[1] chamber and I stood before the seven[2]
judges. But now that the time had come for me to be
sentenced, I was sicker than ever. When the guards

---

[1] **Inquisition**—a court appointed by the Roman Catholic Church in Spain.
From 1480 to 1834 it was under state control. The task of the court was to
discover and severely punish those who disagreed with the teachings of the
Catholic Church. It was particularly severe and cruel in the sixteenth century.

[2] The number seven is often thought to be a magical number. It sometimes
suggests good and sometimes suggests evil.

finally untied me, and I was permitted to sit, I felt that I was going to faint. The sentence—the terrible sentence of death—was the last thing I heard before I felt myself slipping away in a faint.

Although I had fainted, I still partly heard and saw what was happening in the room. The voices of the Inquisition seemed to hum in the air around me. I saw the lips of the black-robed judges, but I could understand nothing. I saw their faces full of anger and firmness as they formed the sylla-

I was to die. The sentence had been read.

bles of my name, and I shuddered. I saw the movement of the heavy black curtains that covered the walls and the seven tall candles upon the table. I turned my head here and there, searching for help— searching for anyone who could save me from this nightmare. But there would be no help from anyone or anything. And then the thought crept into my mind, like the rich note of a musical instrument, of what sweet rest there would be in my grave. I was to die. The sentence had been read. Then—nothing but blackness all around me. Silence, stillness, and night were my universe.

I had fainted, and knew nothing. Suddenly, movement and sound returned. Then a blank pause. Then again, sound, motion, and touch came back to me slowly, and then I was awake once more. At that moment, a feeling of such terror gripped me that I wanted to faint again. I was attacked by memories of the trial, of the judges, of the tall candles, of the sentence, of the sickness, of my fainting.

As these thoughts raced through my mind, I kept my eyes tightly closed. I could tell that I lay upon my back and that I was untied. Cautiously, I reached out my hand and felt something damp and hard. I kept my hand there for several minutes while I tried to imagine what it could be. I longed to open my eyes, but I did not dare. I was desperately afraid of what would happen when I did. It was not that I was afraid to look at horrible sights, I was afraid there would be *nothing* to see.

At length, with a wild despair, I opened my eyes. As soon as I did, I realized that my worst dreams had come true. I could see nothing— nothing but endless blackness. Everything was completely dark. I gasped for breath and felt a terrible fear. The darkness seemed to be squeezing the breath out of me.

The men and women who had been condemned to death at the Inquisition, I knew, were killed at the *autos-da-fé*.[3] One of these had been held on the very

---

[3] *autos-da-fé*—public ceremonies where the condemned were burned at the stake.

night of the day of my trial. Had I been sent to a dark **dungeon**[4] to await the next killing, which would not take place for many months? I knew at once that this could not be true. Victims were always in demand. My **captors**[5] had something else in mind, I knew. But what?

At that moment, another frightening idea occurred to me. Once again, I fainted in terror. When I recovered, I jumped to my feet and waved my arms wildly all around me. I felt nothing, yet I was afraid to move a step for fear that I would touch the walls of a **tomb**.[6] Had they buried me alive? Sweat burst from every pore. Very cautiously, I moved forward with my arms out in front of me. My eyes strained to catch some faint ray of light. I walked several feet but never touched a wall. At last I breathed a sigh of relief. This was not a tomb, I knew. It was far too large. At least I would not suffer that horrible death.

With no plan in mind, I continued to step onward. As I walked, I thought about the horrible

---

[4] **dungeon**—underground room or cell in which prisoners were held.

[5] **captors**—people who have captured a person or thing.

[6] **tomb**—grave or other burial place.

rumors I had heard about Toledo.[7] I'd heard stories that were so terrible they were told only in a whisper. What form of **torture**[8] was in store for me? I had no doubt that I was to die, because that was my sentence. But how would I be killed? And when?

At last, my outstretched hands found a wall that seemed very solid. It was smooth, slimy, and cold. I walked along the wall, stepping carefully, because I still could see nothing. The wall was so smooth that I knew I might be able to walk around the whole cell without ever realizing that I was back at my starting point. Hoping to somehow mark the wall, I reached for the knife I had had in my pocket when I was led into the Inquisition room. It was gone, however, as were my clothes. I was wearing some type of robe made of coarse cotton. I tore a piece from the hem of the robe and placed the cloth at right angles to the wall. I would use this to mark my starting point.

My plan was to walk around the wall of the dungeon, but I had not realized how difficult this would be. The ground was damp and slippery. I

[7] Toledo—city in central Spain, headquarters for the Spanish Inquisition.

[8] **torture**—giving of severe pain as a punishment or as a way of forcing people to do something against their will.

staggered[9] onward for perhaps a half hour, and then I stumbled and fell. As I lay there, exhaustion overcame me. Within minutes, I fell into the deepest of sleeps.

When I awoke, I stretched out an arm and found beside me a loaf of bread and a pitcher of water. I was too tired to think how it had got there, but I was not too tired to eat. I fell upon the meal with a good appetite. Shortly afterwards, I continued my walk around the prison. After what seemed like forever, I came upon the piece of robe. Up to the time when I fell, I had counted fifty-two paces. After my rest, I had walked forty-eight paces more. As best I could calculate, my cell was 100 paces—or fifty yards—around. However, since there were so many angles in the walls, I could form no guess about the shape of my cell.

There was no real reason for doing these measurements, of course. I had no hope of escape, but I was curious, so I knew I would continue. Next I would walk across the dungeon, from one side to another. At first, I moved very carefully. The floor seemed solid, but it was slippery with slime. After a while, however, I became more courageous and began to step firmly. I wanted to cross the dungeon

---

[9] **staggered**—walked unsteadily.

in as straight a line as possible. I had moved forward some ten or twelve paces in this manner when the hem of my robe became tangled around my legs. I stepped on it and fell violently on my face.

In my confusion, I did not immediately understand where I had landed. After a moment or two, however, I suddenly found that although my chin was resting on the floor of the prison, my lips, and the upper portion of my head, touched nothing. At the same time, my forehead was wet with a **clammy vapor**,[10] and I could smell the terrible stink of **decaying**[11] flesh. I put my arm out and shuddered to find that I had fallen at the very edge of a round pit, whose size, of course, I could not know. While I groped around the stone just below the edge of the pit, I was able to dislodge a small rock and let it fall into the pit. For many seconds I listened to it fall against the sides of the pit as it went down. Finally, I heard a distant plunge into the water. At the same moment, I heard a sound like the quick opening

> *I suddenly found that although my chin was resting on the floor of the prison, my lips, and the upper portion of my head, touched nothing.*

---

[10] **clammy vapor**—damp, cold air.
[11] **decaying**—rotting.

and closing of a door overhead, while a faint gleam of light flashed suddenly through the gloom, and just as suddenly faded away.

I now clearly saw the **doom**[12] that had been prepared for me and congratulated myself that I had avoided falling into the terrible pit. One step more, and the world would have seen me no more.

Shaking all over, I crawled back to the wall. I decided I would rather die there than face the terrors of the pit. I could not forget what I had read about these pits, so I knew that the fall itself would be the least of the horrors.

For many hours, I lay crouched against the wall. Later, I stretched out to sleep. When I awoke, I once again found a loaf of bread and a pitcher of water. Terribly thirsty, I drank the water in a gulp. It must have been drugged, for almost immediately I felt drowsy again. A sleep as deep as death came upon me. How long it lasted I do not know but, when I awoke again, the objects around me were now clearer. Thanks to a faint light, I was able to see the walls of the prison.

I had been mistaken about its size. The room was not fifty yards around—it was much closer to twenty-five. How had I made such a mistake in the

---

[12] **doom**—fate or death.

calculations? Eventually, I decided that the mistake had been made because I fainted halfway through my measurements. In my first attempt at exploration, I had counted fifty-two paces, up to the period when I fell. At that point, I must have been within a pace or two of the piece of the robe. I then slept— and, upon awaking, I must have walked around the same area again, thus assuming that the dungeon was nearly double what it actually was. My confusion had blinded me to the true size of the cell.

I had been wrong, too, about the shape of the dungeon. In feeling my way, I had found many angles. I saw now, however, that the room was quite square. The walls were not made of brick but of huge pieces of iron, joined together. Upon the walls the **monks**[13] had painted blurred pictures of weapons of torture, monsters, skeletons, and other horrible beings. With great effort, I turned my eyes away from this terrible art.

All this I observed with great difficulty, for my position had been changed while I slept. I now lay upon my back, and at full length, on a low wooden frame. I was tied tightly to the frame with a long

---

[13] **monks**—men who give up all worldly things and lead lives of religious duty.

rope. Only my head and left arm remained untied. My arm was free, I knew, so that I could eat with great effort from the dish of salty food that had been put at my side. I finished the food quickly and then saw to my horror that there was no water with this meal. Although my thirst was terrible, I soon noticed something else.

On the ceiling, some forty feet above, was a painted figure of Father Time.[14] He held what looked like a huge **pendulum**,[15] like the kind found on old clocks. Something about the pendulum caught my eye as I stared upwards. When I stared harder, I saw that the pendulum, which was directly above me, was moving. Its sweep was brief and, of course, slow. I watched it for some minutes, somewhat in fear, but more in wonder. Tired at last of its dull movement, I turned my eyes to the other objects in my cell.

A slight noise attracted my notice. I looked to the floor and saw several enormous rats running across it. They had come up from the pit, which lay just within view to my right. Even now, while I looked, they came up in troops, hurriedly, with hungry eyes. They were large, black rats—larger

---

[14] Pictures of Father Time usually show a bald, bearded old man. He is often holding a water jar, an hourglass, or a scythe, which is a tool used to cut grass or wheat.

[15] **pendulum**—weight hung at a central point so that it is free to swing back and forth. A tall clock is often timed by a pendulum.

and blacker than any I had ever seen. Their tiny eyes glowed in the dark, and I could see their whiskers twitching at the scent of my food. With much effort, I scared them away.

Because I had escaped death in the pit, I would be cut to shreds by a huge, swinging pendulum.

It might have been half an hour, or perhaps even an hour, before I again looked upward. What I then saw puzzled me greatly. The sweep of the pendulum had increased in length by nearly a yard. Because of this, its speed was also much greater. But what worried me most was that it looked lower than it had been before. I could plainly see that the pendulum, which was made of a kind of steel, had a bottom edge that was as sharp as a razor. I could hear the hiss this deadly blade made as it sliced through the air. Now I understood the plan my jailers had in mind for me. Because I had escaped death in the pit, I would be cut to shreds by a huge, swinging pendulum.

There's no point in telling of the long, long hours I lay there watching the swing of the pendulum. In terror, I watched it inch its way down towards me. Many days passed before it swept so closely over me that it fanned the air over my chest. The smell of the sharp steel forced itself into my nostrils. When I could think, I prayed for it all to be over. In my most **frantic**[16] moments, I even tried to force myself upwards toward the terrible blade. At last, I was suddenly calm and lay smiling at it, like a child with a glittering toy.

Although I was nearly overcome with fear during this time, I still **craved**[17] food and water. With painful effort, I stretched my left arm as far as the ropes permitted and grabbed hold of the small pieces of food that the rats left me. As I put some to my mouth, I suddenly felt a little hope. Yet what business had I with hope? I was a fool, an idiot. But still, I felt hope.

The pendulum had been set up at a right angle to my length to cross the region of my heart. It would first slice through my robe and then begin slicing through skin. Down, steadily down it crept. Its sweep was now about thirty feet. I took a terrible pleasure in watching it swing left, then right, never stopping. I laughed and then I howled as the pendulum moved closer.

Down it swung until it came within three inches of my chest. I struggled violently—furiously—to free

---

[16] **frantic**—wild.
[17] **craved**—deeply desired.

my left arm, which was tied at the elbow. If I could have freed the entire arm, I would have tried to grab the pendulum and stop its deadly swing. But I could not work it free of the ropes.

Down—still **inevitably**[18] down the pendulum swung! I gasped and struggled and shrunk back at its every sweep. My eyes followed its back-and-forth movement though they closed when it came down. I would have welcomed death at this point. Anything was better than this horrible waiting!

Finally, I saw that some ten or twelve more minutes would bring the steel in actual contact with my robe. When I saw this, I was overcome with the clear, collected calmness of **despair**.[19] And yet, I could not stop hoping. For the first time in many hours, many days, I *thought*. Was it possible that the blade would cut through the rope on my chest first, thereby allowing me a moment or two to jump free? With a burst of energy, I pulled my head up and looked carefully at the ropes. My jailers had been far too careful, I saw with a glance. The ropes crossed my body in all directions, except over the portion of my chest that would be cut open by the pendulum.

---

[18] **inevitably**—unavoidably.

[19] **despair**—feeling of total defeat.

In despair, I dropped my head back. As I lay there again, another idea came to me. Once again, I dared to hope. Perhaps the rats would be my answer. Could I use these wild, starving rats to save me? The whole time I lay upon the frame, the rats had been watching me, their red eyes glaring as they waited to make a feast of my shredded body. "What food," I wondered, "have they been eating in the pit these many years?"

The whole time I lay upon the frame, the rats had been watching me, their red eyes glaring as they waited to make a feast of my shredded body.

In spite of my best efforts, the rats had eaten all but a bit of the food in my dish. I quickly rubbed my hand over the inside of the dish and coated my palm with the greasy, spicy juices left over from the meat. Then, without hesitating, I rubbed the rest of the juices all over the ropes that I could reach. Then I lay breathlessly still.

At first, the hungry animals were startled and frightened at the change. They saw that I had stopped chasing them away but couldn't understand why. But they only hesitated for a moment. The boldest of the pack jumped upon the framework and sniffed at the ropes. This seemed a signal for a general rush. They came out of the pit in groups and leapt upon me. Hundreds of rats sniffing, crawling, **gnawing**[20] upon me. They pressed, they swarmed, they covered me in heaps. They climbed upon my throat and their cold lips touched my own. A disgust that has no name swelled in my chest and chilled my heart. Yet one more minute, and the struggle would be over. I could plainly feel that the ropes were looser. The rats were gnawing through them, and I would be free. Keeping my eyes shut against the horror, I lay completely still.

Hundreds of rats sniffing, crawling, gnawing upon me. They pressed, they swarmed, they covered me in heaps.

At length, I felt that I was free. The ropes hung in ribbons from my body. But the stroke of the pendulum had already cut through my robe and was pressing against my chest. Twice more it swung, and a sharp pain shot through me. But the moment of escape had arrived. With a cautious sideways movement, I scared the rats away and slid off the framework. For the moment, at least, I was free.

Free!—and in the grasp of the Inquisition! As soon as I stepped away from my wooden bed of

[20] **gnawing**—chewing.

horror, the motion of the hellish pendulum stopped. I watched as it was drawn up through the ceiling by some invisible force. So here was another lesson for me. Every movement was watched.

And yet—I was free! But free to do what? Had I escaped one death only to be delivered to another? With that thought I rolled my eyes nervously around the iron walls. Something unusual had taken place in my cell, but at first I could not see what it was. For many minutes, I looked about without seeing. And then it dawned on me. There was now a half-inch crack between the walls and floor of the prison, and coming from the crack was a bright light that lit the whole cell! Try as I might, I could not see a thing through the crack. But still it was clear to me—the floor had completely separated from the walls. I knew it as well as I knew myself!

Unreal! As I looked wildly about, the smell of hot iron rose to my nostrils. The colors of the paintings on the wall glowed. Demon eyes stared at me from every direction. I panted! I gasped for breath! There could be no doubt what my torturers planned for me now. Oh! Those cruel judges! Those evil men! I shrank from the glowing walls to the coolness of the pit in the center of the cell. I rushed to its deadly edge and prepared to jump in. Anything would be better than the burning walls. After a moment, though, I realized my mistake. The glare from the roof showed that the pit was filled with rats and decay and horror. How foolish I had been! Oh! Any horror but this! Fool, why didn't I realize that into the pit was where my jailers wished me to go? With a shriek, I rushed away from the edge and buried my face in my hands, weeping bitterly.

The heat rapidly increased, and once again I looked up. There had been a second change in the cell—and now the change was obviously in its shape. With a low rumble, the room, that had once been square, had shifted its form into that of an oval. The burning walls, it seemed, were pushing me towards the pit. "Death," I said, "any death but that of the pit!"

Still the walls kept pushing inward. The heat was unbearable. At length, there was only an inch or so for my burned and scarred body to stand on. I struggled no more, but let out one loud, long, and final scream of despair. I staggered upon the **brink**.[21] I closed my eyes—

---

[21] **brink**—edge.

And suddenly, there was a loud blast as of many trumpets! There was a hum of human voices! There was a harsh grating as of a thousand thunders! The burning walls rushed back! An outstretched arm caught my own as I fell, fainting, into the pit. It was the arm of General Lasalle.[22] The French army had entered Toledo. The Inquisition was in the hands of its enemies. I was saved!

THE END

---

[22] General Lasalle—leader of the French army at the time of the Spanish Inquisition.

The Masque of the Red Death

This story, published in 1842, is set in the Middle Ages. As a result of the Red Death, a deadly disease that scholars now believe was originally spread by rats, more than half of Prince Prospero's kingdom lies dead. Rather than try to help, however, the prince decides to shut himself in with a thousand friends and live in luxury.

The "Red Death" had been destroying the country for a long time. No **pestilence**[1] had ever been so fatal or so hideous. Blood was everywhere—bright red blood that stained the body, clothes, and bed sheets of the victims. There were sharp pains and sudden dizziness and then terrible bleeding. The

---

[1] **pestilence**—deadly disease.

disease was so rapid and so severe that its victims were dead within thirty minutes of spilling the first drop of blood.

Prince Prospero, who was happy and rich and mad at the thought of all these people dying, decided that something must be done. After more than half his kingdom had died, Prospero called to his castle 1,000 of the most cheerful and healthy men and women of

Prospero and his fellow courtiers were well-fed and safe from the Red Death. The outside world would take care of itself.

his court. With these, he moved into an **abbey**[2] that was surrounded by a strong, high wall that had iron gates. Once Prospero and his **courtiers**[3] were safe inside the abbey, the servants slammed the gates and welded them shut. The courtiers decided that no one would be able to enter or leave the abbey. Prospero and his fellow courtiers were well-fed and safe from the Red Death. The outside world would take care of itself. In the meantime, it was a mistake to be sad or to think.

Prospero had supplied the abbey with everything 1,001 people could need. More important, he had made sure that there would be plenty of

---

[2] **abbey**—building like one belonging to a church.
[3] **courtiers**—members of a ruler's court.

entertainment for himself and his guests. There were clowns and jesters and actors and ballet dancers. There were musicians, there were beautiful women, and there was plenty of wine. All these and security were within the abbey. Outside the abbey was the Red Death.

For six months, Prospero's thousand friends in the abbey enjoyed themselves. At the end of the sixth month, Prospero decided to celebrate by holding a **masked ball**.[4] The ball, he said, would be the most magnificent anyone had ever seen.

It was a wild scene, that ball. But first, let me tell about the rooms where it was held. Seven rooms were used. One room led into another, and the seven together formed an almost perfect circle. But because of the odd angles in the walls, it was impossible to see more than one room at a time. In each room, there were two tall and narrow Gothic windows[5] that looked out upon the hallway. Each window was of a stained glass that matched exactly the color of the room. So, for example, in the blue room, which was the first of the seven, there hung

---

[4] **masked ball**—party at which people dress up, wear masks, and dance.

[5] Gothic windows—windows with pointed arches.

blue stained-glass windows. The second room was purple, with purple windows. The third was green, and the fourth was orange. The fifth was all white, and the sixth was violet. The walls of the seventh room were covered in black velvet tapestries that hung all over the ceiling and down the walls. In this room only, the color of the windows did not match the color of the room. In this room, the window panes were red—a deep blood-red color.

There were no lamps or candles in any of the rooms. Instead, the rooms were lit from outside in. Huge braziers of fire[6] on three-legged stands stood in the hallway outside, opposite each window, so that the light shone inward into the room. This lighting made the first six rooms look strange and fantastic. But the seventh room, with the firelight coming through the red windows, looked strange in a horrible way, as if blood were flowing into the room through the windows. The faces of people who went in the room looked so wild that most of the guests were afraid to step into it.

In the seventh room stood a gigantic clock made of fine, black wood. Its **pendulum**[7] swung to and fro with a dull, heavy clang. When the clock struck,

---

[6] braziers of fire—metal fireplaces.

[7] **pendulum**—weight hung at a central point so that it is free to swing back and forth. A tall clock is often timed by a pendulum.

it made such a loud, **peculiar**[8] sound that the musicians of the orchestra stopped their playing to hear. This caused the dancers to stop dancing and the crowd to stop murmuring. The giddy men and women stopped their chatting and grew pale, and the oldest in the crowd passed their hands over their brows and looked confused the entire time the chimes rang.

But, in spite of the clock and the room colored by blood, the **masquerade**[9] was a wonderful success. Prospero himself had directed the preparations for the ball. He created **grotesque**[10] costumes for his guests and hung decorations that looked as if they were invented by a madman. If the masquerade looked like a dream—with its strange colors and its glare and glitter—then the guests themselves looked like something out of a nightmare. They wore costumes of the oddest colors and fabrics. For much of the night, they wandered through the first six rooms, commenting on the colors and the strangeness of everyone's appearance.

---

[8] **peculiar**—strange.
[9] **masquerade**—party at which people wear masks and other disguises.
[10] **grotesque**—ugly, unnatural.

In the hours before midnight, the guests danced and drank and gossiped. And then, at the stroke of midnight, all were silent except the ebony clock. As the clock rang, the dancers listened uneasily. Before the echo of the last ring faded, a few noticed a masked figure that had not been present before. These few whispered to others, who told others and others until it seemed that the whole ball was buzzing about the stranger.

His gown was dripping with blood, and his mask was sprinkled with what looked like the blood of the Red Death.

As the masked figure moved slowly into the blue room, the guests had a chance to look carefully at him. Everyone felt that his costume was beyond a joke. He was tall and thin and covered in a burial **shroud**.[11] The mask that hid his face looked exactly like that of a stiffened **corpse**.[12] Even so, in this crowd of fantastic costumes, the stranger might have gone unnoticed but for one thing: his gown was dripping with blood, and his mask was sprinkled with what looked like the blood of the Red Death.

---

[11] **shroud**—covering of cloth for the dead.
[12] **corpse**—dead body.

When Prince Prospero saw this strange figure, he shivered with fear and horror. Then, just as quickly, he pulled himself tall with a look of rage upon his face.

"Who dares appear here like this?" Prospero demanded. "Who dares to insult us by wearing a costume of the Red Death? Seize[13] this man and take off his mask so that we know who to hang when the sun rises!"

> **"Seize this man and take off his mask so that we know who to hang when the sun rises!"**

Prospero made this command in the blue room. His words rang throughout the seven rooms loudly and clearly. As soon as they heard Prospero's command, a group of guests rushed towards the figure, but no one wanted to get close enough to touch him. So they stopped short and let him pass. The whole company shrank from the centers of the rooms to the walls. The masked figure brushed by Prospero and moved through the blue room to the purple—through the purple to the green—through the green to the orange—through this again to the white—and then to the violet. No one tried to stop him.

---

[13] **Seize**—take hold of suddenly, grasp.

As the **intruder**[14] was passing through the violet room and into the black room, Prospero, mad with rage and shame for his own fear, sprang into action. He raced through the six rooms with a **dagger**[15] in his hand. Fear stopped everyone from following him. Prospero caught up with the intruder in the black room, the room that so terrified all 1,000 guests. When Prospero came within three or four feet of the intruder's bloody cloak, the tall figure suddenly turned around and faced the prince for the first time. There was a sharp cry, and then the dagger dropped gleaming upon the black carpet. On top of the dagger fell Prospero, who was dead before his body hit the carpet.

When the guests saw what had happened, they threw themselves at the tall figure. They were horrified to find that under the cloak and mask there was no man or woman—nothing.

At that moment, the guests understood that the Red Death was among them. He had come like a thief in the night. And one by one the guests dropped in bloody heaps upon the floor and died in

---

[14] **intruder**—unwelcome visitor.

[15] **dagger**—short sword used for stabbing.

despair as they fell. When the last guest fell, the ebony clock stopped ticking and the flames in the braziers went out forever. And Darkness and Decay and the Red Death had power over all.

THE END

The Fall of the House of Usher

Poe loved to write about madness. In "The Fall of the House of Usher" (1839), Roderick Usher appears to have lost his sanity well before the story begins. But has he? The unnamed narrator of the story must find a way to keep his own sanity while on a visit to the terrifying House of Usher.

On a dull, dark, and silent day in the fall, when the heavy clouds hung low in the heavens, I was riding alone, on horseback, through a very boring part of the country. Eventually I found myself, as evening approached, near the **melancholy**[1] House of Usher.

---

[1] **melancholy**—gloomy; very sad.

I didn't know a thing about the House of Usher at the time, but the minute I saw it, a horrible sense of gloom and darkness came over me. I looked at the scene before me—the house, the simple path leading up to it, the vacant windows, and the dying trees—and I felt a kind of **despair**[2] that I've never felt before. I felt sick at heart, but I did not understand why.

What was it that so frightened me when I looked at the House of Usher?

What was it? I wondered. What was it that so frightened me when I looked at the House of Usher? It was a mystery that I could not begin to understand, yet my fear was very real.

Then I wondered whether a different arrangement of the house and grounds would take away the sadness and fear. I rode my horse to the steep banks of a mountain lake in front of the house, and looked at the reflections of the view. But this frightened me even more. How I longed to turn and ride in the opposite direction! Even so, I directed my horse toward the house and made my way slowly through the mist. I had no choice, as the House of Usher was my **destination**.[3] I had

---

[2] **despair**—deep, unbearable sadness.

[3] **destination**—place to which a traveler is going.

been invited here by its owner, one of my boyhood friends, Roderick Usher.

Usher had sent me a letter—a wild letter begging me to come—that I felt I must reply to in person. In his letter, he spoke of a terrible illness of body that kept him in the house and a mental illness that caused him great confusion. He wanted to see me, he said, because I was his best, his only personal friend. If I would come, he said, it would cheer him. He sounded desperate in his letter, so I packed my bags quickly and made preparations to go.

Although as boys we were very good friends, I hadn't seen Roderick Usher for years. He had been a shy child who spoke only when he absolutely had to. His parents were quiet and withdrawn, like him, although I knew they had had a reputation for kindness and generosity. The Ushers kept to themselves, however, so it was no surprise that I hadn't heard from the son for many years.

In his letter, Usher explained that he had never married or had children. He was the last of the Ushers, he said, and the family name would die when he died. I considered that perhaps this was the reason that he was feeling so desperate and unhappy.

As I rode toward the house, I again allowed my imagination to run wild. A **murky**[4] gray mist surrounded the house, separating it from the rest of the world. The house itself was very old. It had been badly stained by age and a type of **fungus**[5] that covered it and had caused the stones of the building to crumble in places.

Adding to the general look of decay was a barely visible crack in the stone that began at the roof. It went in a zigzag fashion, all the way down the front of the house to the dark and murky mountain lake that **lapped**[6] up against the stone. The lake, which was as black as night, was undoubtedly the source of the mist that hung over the house.

I noted all of these things as I rode slowly over a short bridge that ended at the front door. A waiting servant took my horse and led me into a **Gothic**[7] archway that led to the entrance hall. Here I was met by a **valet**,[8] who silently led me through many dark passageways toward the room of his master. Much that I saw on my strange tour added to my nervousness—the carvings on the ceiling, the dark

---

[4] **murky**—dark and foggy or smoky looking; shadowy and thick.

[5] **fungus**—small plant that lives by absorbing the dead material in which it grows.

[6] **lapped**—gently splashed.

[7] **Gothic**—style of architecture that uses pointed arches and fine stone carving.

[8] **valet**—man's servant.

tapestries[9] on the walls, the endless blackness of the floors, and the fantastic prizes and coats of arms that rattled as I passed by. I had been used to such things from childhood. Why did they make me think that I was going somewhere that no one in his right mind would ever want to go?

On one of the staircases, I met the family doctor. I thought his face had a look of **sly**[10] confusion. He seemed to look at me fearfully and to want to speak to me, but the valet hurried on. The valet now threw open a door and ushered me into his master's room.

The room in which I found myself was very large. The windows were long, narrow, and pointed. They were so high off the floor that it would have been impossible for me to touch even the lowest part of the window sill. Weak light made its way in through the window panes, but because the room was so large, the light never touched the shadows in every corner. Dark draperies hung upon the walls. The furniture was uncomfortable, old, and torn. Many books and musical instruments were

---

[9] tapestries—fabrics with pictures and designs woven in and hung on walls.

[10] **sly**—secret, sneaky.

scattered here and there. The room, I decided in an instant, was the gloomiest I had ever seen.

Upon my entrance, Usher rose from a sofa on which he had been lying. He greeted me with a lively warmth that I at first thought was overdone. A glance at his face, however, told me otherwise. He was truly happy to have me here. After this greeting, we sat down and studied each other in silence.

As I looked at him, I felt a terrible sense of pity mixed with awe. How could a man have changed so much in such a short period of time?

As I looked at him, I felt a terrible sense of pity mixed with **awe**.[11] How could a man have changed so much in such a short period of time? I couldn't believe that this pale man was my childhood friend. But his face had always been remarkable. He had a pale, thin face, with large eyes. His lips were thin and pale, but had a beautiful curve. His chin was well-shaped but weak, his forehead high. What startled me was his paleness and the glitter in his eyes. His hair was fine and floated like a web around his face. Worse yet was my friend's manner. He simply could not sit still. His

---

[11] **awe**—a strong feeling of wonder.

hands moved, his feet jerked, his eyes shifted—all in a nervous **agitation**[12] that was terrible to watch. His speaking voice was nearly as odd as his manner. At times he shouted, at times he whispered, and at times he spoke in a complete **monotone**.[13]

At this first meeting, Usher spoke of his strong desire to see me and the comfort he expected that I would bring to him. He also tried to explain his illness, although his explanation made very little sense. His illness, he said, had affected his whole family, and there was no possible cure. He immediately added that it was just a case of nerves that would soon pass. For the most part, the illness caused the victim to be extremely sensitive to the five senses—sight, sound, taste, touch, and smell. Usher could only eat the **blandest**[14] of foods. He could wear clothes only of certain textures. He could not stand to have a single flower in the room, and even a little light bothered his eyes. Most sounds irritated him greatly, and he could listen to no music except that made by a stringed instrument.

Worst of all, he lived in terrible fear of what was to come. "I dread the events of the future," he said,

---

[12] **agitation**—violent moving or shaking.

[13] **monotone**—sameness of tone, without a change of pitch.

[14] **blandest**—plainest, most unflavored.

"not in themselves, but in their results. My fears overwhelm me to the point that some day soon, I know I will give in to them. I must give up life and reason together in my struggle with fear."

Usher believed that he was unable to leave his house. For years he had stayed indoors, within its walls, and had no idea of what went on in the outside world. He admitted, however, that although he had been ill for years, something more had led him to feel so desperate these last few weeks. His beloved sister, his only companion for long years, his last relative on Earth, was also very ill and would die soon. "Her death," he said, with a bitterness that I will never forget, would leave him "a hopeless, sickly man—the last of the long race of Usher."

While he spoke, the lady Madeline (for so she was called) passed slowly through the other end of the room and, without noticing my presence, disappeared. I looked at Madeline with astonishment and dread, although I couldn't explain why I would have these feelings. My eyes followed her as she walked across the room, and then I stared for a moment or two at the door that she had closed behind her. When I turned to her brother again, I saw that he had buried his face in his hands and that a trickle of tears had seeped out between his pale and bony fingers.

I later learned that the disease of the lady Madeline had long **baffled**[15] her doctors. She had been gradually wasting away for years, although no one could find out why. The night before I arrived, she had finally taken to her bed and was too weak to get up again. The glimpse I had had of her would probably be my last. In fact, Usher said, it was very likely that I would never see the lady again.

For the next several days of my visit, Usher didn't mention his sister. During these days, I spent most of my time trying to cheer the poor man. We painted and read together or I listened while he played wild music on his guitar. Although at times he seemed fairly calm, I could tell that my presence really had very little effect on him. His mood was gloomy and dark at all times during the day. It became darker still each evening when night began to fall.

I will always remember the many quiet hours I spent alone with the master of the House of Usher. His long, **improvised**[16] musical pieces will forever

---

[15] **baffled**—puzzled.
[16] **improvised**—made up.

ring in my ears. How could I forget the sound of his dark, endless playing? And how could I ever forget the sight of that strange room, with its dark draperies and Usher's fantastic, frightening paintings upon the wall? One such painting stays with me night and day. It was a small picture of an immensely long and rectangular tunnel or **vault**.[17] The walls of the vault were smooth and white, although it was clear that the vault pictured was far underground. No light source could be seen in the painting, although the tunnel was filled with a vast amount of light that bathed the whole in a **ghastly**[18] and unlikely light.

> *And how could I ever forget the sight of that strange room, with its dark draperies and Usher's fantastic, frightening paintings upon the wall?*

I have just spoken of Usher's guitar playing, and yet I feel that I must say more. The musical pieces that he composed for this instrument were quite odd. He played these pieces with a strange energy that I found difficult to watch. Listening to the pieces was even more difficult. Many times, as

---

[17] **vault**—underground passage or room; a tomb.
[18] **ghastly**—horrible, shocking.

he played, he recited bizarre rhymes that showed his excitement about the music.

I remember one of these poems quite well, although I would prefer to forget it. The poem was called "The Haunted Palace." It was about a beautiful palace in a green and lovely valley. After years of happiness, the palace is suddenly overcome by sorrow. At the end of the poem, a hideous crowd of laughing spirits attacks the palace and haunts the people who live there.

How well I remember the discussions we would have whenever Usher recited "The Haunted Palace." I cannot tell of the wildness of his ideas. He believed that all vegetation—trees, plants, and flowers—had intelligence. The fungus that covered his house, then, he thought of as a living, breathing thing that was capable of a full range of thoughts and feelings. The decayed trees, the mountain lake, the mist—all of it was as alive as any human. It had all molded his family and made *him* what he was. Opinions like this need no comment, and I will make none.

Usher's collection of books was as strange as his paintings and his music. Every book in his library had as its subject the strange, the fantastic, the **supernatural**,[19] and all other types of oddities.

[19] **supernatural**—above or beyond what is natural. For example, ghosts are supernatural.

Usher would spend hours dreaming over these volumes, and I wonder what effect their grimness had on his mental state.

One evening, after I had been at the house for perhaps two weeks, Usher told me rather suddenly that his sister Madeline had died. Without pausing, he explained that he intended to keep her corpse for two weeks or more within one of the vaults that were under the main part of the building. He decided to do this, he said, because he wanted to give her doctors a chance to examine her body in a search for clues about her illness. I could not argue with this decision. Also, I remembered the strange doctor I had met on the stairs on my first day here.

At Usher's request, I helped him prepare for the temporary burial of his sister. After her body was placed in a **coffin**[20] by the servants, he and I carried the coffin down to the area under the house. The vault in which we placed it was small, damp, and entirely without light. It had been used, apparently, in past times, as a type of terrible **dungeon**[21] for prisoners. Later, it also had been used to store

---

[20] **coffin**—box into which a dead person is put to be buried.

[21] **dungeon**—dark underground room or cell in which prisoners are held.

gunpowder. Because of this, any cracks in the vault had been carefully sealed. The huge iron door, when closed, formed a tight seal with the door frame.

Once we had arranged the coffin on the floor, we partially unscrewed its top and looked upon the face of Madeline. I was immediately struck with how similar she and her brother looked. Usher, who perhaps understood what I was thinking, murmured something about the two of them being twins, which had given them a special bond when she was alive.

Once we had arranged the coffin on the floor, we partially unscrewed its top and looked upon the face of Madeline.

Although she had been sick for many years, Madeline looked astonishingly well lying in her coffin. There was even a slight blush on her cheeks, and her lips were parted in a small death smile that I stared at with some fascination. Soon, we replaced the lid and screwed it down and then set about the difficult process of shutting the huge iron door of the vault. Because the door was so heavy, we had a great deal of difficulty moving it. When we finally closed it, its great weight caused an unusually sharp grating sound as it moved upon its hinges. After we had the door shut tight, we made our way back up the corridors and stairs to Usher's less gloomy rooms.

For several days afterwards, Usher wept and grieved. And then one day, a change came over him. His ordinary manner had vanished. His ordinary hobbies, such as reading and painting, were neglected or forgotten. He roamed from room to room with hurried steps, back and forth, back and forth. His horribly pale skin became paler still, and any light that had once shined in his eyes was gone. He spoke only in a whisper now, and I could hear his voice shaking. Day after day, he roamed the house, searching for something, or he stood, staring into space, listening for something. It's not surprising that his condition frightened me. I felt his strange concerns were taking me over. I, too, began to feel nervous and was constantly checking to see who was in the room behind me.

It was, I believe, the seventh or eighth night after placing the lady Madeline in the vault that I became unbearably frightened. As I was preparing for bed that night, I felt extremely nervous. For hours I lay awake struggling with my feelings of fear. I heard the noise of curtains rustling on the walls and the bed. A storm was blowing outside, and I became more and more alarmed. As I lay there shaking, I became aware of a strange series of sounds somewhere within the house. Almost overcome with panic, I threw on my clothes and began pacing rapidly to and fro in my room.

I had taken just a few turns across the room when I heard someone climbing the staircase near my room. A moment later, I heard a light rap on the door, and Usher entered with a lamp in his hand. His face was, as usual, terribly pale—but I saw in his eyes a **hysteria**[22] that I had never seen before.

"Have you seen it?" he asked abruptly, after looking around for some moments in silence. "You have not seen it? Well, then wait! You shall!"

"Have you seen it?" he asked abruptly, after looking around for some moments in silence. "You have not seen it? Well, then wait! You shall!" After saying this, he hurried over to the window and threw it open. The storm that had been raging for hours rushed in and nearly lifted us off our feet. It was a wild storm, yet I saw a strange beauty in the

---

[22] **hysteria**—unrestrained excitement or emotion.

night. The heavy clouds hung low and the wind beat against the roof. The moon and the stars were hidden by the clouds, but we could not see any flashes of lightning. And yet the mist that surrounded the house glowed with a strange light that I could not explain.

"You must not—you shall not look at this!" I said, with a shiver and led Usher away from the window. "This strange light, which frightens you so, has something to do with the storm and its effect on the mountain lake. Let's close the window, and then I will read one of your favorite books to you. We'll sit together for the rest of this terrible night."

The book that I picked up and started to read from was called *Mad Tryst*,[23] by Sir Launcelot Canning. I called it Usher's favorite as a joke. The book was a love story, which Usher normally did not care for, but I hoped that it would distract him.

Usher sat silently as I read. Eventually, I arrived at the well-known portion of the story where Ethelred, the hero of the story, has to force his way into the cave

---

[23] *Tryst*—meeting or date between lovers.

"You must not—you shall not look at this!" I said, with a shiver and led Usher away from the window.

of a **hermit**.[24] Right in the middle of my reading, I was interrupted by a small sound that seemed to be coming from the other end of the house. I stopped to listen and then decided that the storm outside had made the sound. So I continued reading.

After another two pages or so, I once again was forced to stop. This time there could be no doubt. From somewhere in the house there came a distant, but harsh, grating sound that sent shivers up my spine. Although I was terribly frightened by this new sound, I said nothing because I did not want to disturb my companion. He had not spoken the whole time I had been reading, but I noticed now that his lips were moving, as if he were whispering to himself. He had slowly moved his chair until he was facing the door. His head had dropped upon his chest, and he was slowly rocking from side to side.

After watching him for a moment or two, I decided to continue with the story. I read another page and then stopped a third time. This time I stopped to listen to a hollow, **metallic**[25] clanging

---

[24] **hermit**—person who leaves society and lives alone.
[25] **metallic**—harsh sound like metal hitting metal.

sound that seemed to be moving in this direction. Completely terrified now, I jumped to my feet. Usher went on gently rocking. I moved towards him and put my hand upon his shoulder. I felt a strong shudder pass over his whole person. There was a sickly smile upon his lips, and I saw that he spoke to himself in a low, hurried whisper. Bending closely over him, I was able to hear what he was saying:

"Not hear it? Yes, I hear it, and have heard it. Long, long, long minutes, many hours, many days, I have heard it! And yet I dared not—oh, pity me, miserable man that I am! I dared not—I dared not speak! We have put her alive in the tomb! You know that my hearing is very sharp. I heard her moving in her coffin. I heard her movements many days ago, yet I dared not speak! And now, tonight, the breaking of her coffin and the grating of the iron door of her prison, and her struggles in the hallway of the vault! Oh where shall I go? Is she coming for me? Is she coming to punish me for burying her alive? I have heard her footsteps on the stair! I have heard the heavy and horrible beating of her heart!

"You, sir," he screamed, turning to me at last, "you are the MADMAN!" With these words, he sprang to his feet and shrieked, "MAD-MAN! I TELL YOU THAT SHE NOW STANDS OUTSIDE THE DOOR!"

Suddenly, the huge door at which Usher was pointing swung slowly back. And there, standing outside the door, *did* stand the **enshrouded**[26] figure of the lady Madeline of Usher. There was blood on her white robes and the marks of some terrible strug-gle upon every portion of her thin body. For a moment she remained trembling in the doorway, then, with a low moaning cry, fell heavily inward upon her brother, and in her violent and now final death agonies, pushed him to the floor, a corpse—a victim to the horrors he had been expecting all along.

> *There was blood on her white robes and the marks of some terrible struggle upon every portion of her thin body.*

From that room, and from that house, I fled in terror. The storm was still raging as I ran across the bridge. Suddenly along the path there was a bolt of wild light that came from somewhere behind me. I turned and stared in wonder at the house. The light, which came from a full, blood-red moon, drew my

---

[26] **enshrouded**—covered in burial cloths.

attention again to the zigzag crack that traveled the house from roof to foundation. I saw now that the light was shining *through* the crack. As I watched, the crack slowly widened, allowing huge gusts of wind to whip through the two parts of the house. There was a terrible shouting sound, like the sound of a thousand rushing rivers, and the mighty walls of the house slowly collapsed inward and began to sink. Then I watched as the waters of the deep, dark lake closed silently over the fragments of the House of Usher.

THE END

The Tell-Tale Heart

In Poe's famous story "The Tell-Tale Heart" (1843), the narrator decides he has no choice but to kill a helpless old man because he has the eye of a vulture.

It is true! I am nervous—I am very, very nervous. But why do you call me mad? The disease has made me think clearly. Above all else, my hearing is perfect. I hear all things in the heaven and on the Earth. I have heard many things in hell. How, then, am I mad? Listen to how calmly I can tell my story.

I can't remember when I first had the idea about the old man. But once I thought of it, it haunted me night and day. I loved the old man. He had never hurt me or caused me trouble. He was rich, but

I had no desire for his gold. So I think it was his eye. Yes, it was his eye! One of his eyes looked like the eye of a **vulture**.[1] It was pale blue, with a film over it. Whenever he looked at me, my blood ran cold. So I made up my mind to kill the old man, and thus rid myself of the evil eye forever.

One of his eyes looked like the eye of a vulture. It was pale blue, with a film over it.

You think I am crazy, but madmen know nothing. No, I was not mad at all. I was careful—oh, so careful. I was very kind to the man in the week before I killed him. And every night, about midnight, I turned the knob of his door and opened it—oh, so gently! And then, when I had made an opening large enough for my head, I inched a covered **lantern**[2] into the room so quietly that he never heard me. I moved the lantern slowly—very, very slowly. I did not want to disturb the old man's sleep. It took me an hour to move my head far enough into the room so that I could see him in his bed. Ha! Would a madman have been as careful as this?

---

[1] **vulture**—large, dark bird of prey that eats mainly the flesh of dead animals.
[2] **lantern**—candle in a metal and glass case.

And then, when my head was far enough into the room, I uncovered the lantern cautiously—oh, so cautiously. I opened it just enough so that a single thin ray of light fell upon the vulture eye. And this I did for seven long nights, every night just at midnight. But I found the eye always closed. And every morning, when the sun came up, I went boldly into his bedroom, and spoke kindly to him, calling him by name in a cheerful tone, and asking how he had slept.

On the eighth night, I was more careful than ever when I opened the door. On this night, I knew that triumph was near. There he lay, fast asleep. He knew nothing of my secret plan, of course, and I chuckled to myself as I inched the door open even further. Perhaps he heard me. He moved suddenly in the bed, as if startled. Did he sense me there? His room was as black as night, so I knew that he could not see me. Slowly, slowly, I kept opening the door a little wider, a little wider.

I had my head in and was about to open the lantern, when my thumb slipped on the latch, and the old man sprang up in bed, crying out: "Who's there?"

I kept quiet. For another hour I did not move a muscle, and in the meantime I did not hear him lie down. He was still sitting up in the bed listening, just as I have listened, night after night after night to the death-watch beetles[3] in the wall.

Eventually I heard a quiet groan, and I knew it was the groan of **mortal terror**.[4] It was not a groan of pain or grief—oh, no!—it was the low quiet sound that arises from the bottom of the soul when a terrible fear overcomes you. Oh yes, I know this sound, because I have made it myself in the middle of the night! I knew what the old man was feeling, and I pitied him, although I smiled at heart. I knew that he had been lying awake ever since the first slight noise, when he had turned in the bed. His fears had been growing since that moment. He had been trying to calm himself, saying, "It is nothing but the wind in the chimney," or "It is only a mouse crossing the floor." But somehow he knew better. Yes, he knew that Death, with his black shadow in front of him, was nearby, and he felt that I was in the room.

---

[3] death-watch beetles—beetles that make a ticking sound as they bore through wood.

[4] **mortal terror**—deadly fear.

When I had waited a long time, very patiently, without hearing him lie down, I decided to open the lantern a little. You cannot imagine how slowly, slowly, I did this, until a single dim ray of light, like the thread of the spider, shot from out the opening and fell full upon the vulture eye. The eye was open— wide, wide open—and I grew angry as I looked at it. I saw it perfectly. It was a dull blue, with a **hideous**[5] film over it that made me sick at heart.

What I heard now was a low, dull, quick sound, the sound of a watch wrapped in cotton.

Now, again, you may call me mad. But I will say again that I am not mad. It is just that my hearing is very, very good. It is better than any other human's on Earth. What I heard now was a low, dull, quick sound, the sound of a watch wrapped in cotton. I knew that sound well, too. It was the beating of the old man's heart. The sound made me even more angry, just as the beating of the drum makes the soldier braver.

But still I kept quiet. I barely breathed. I held the lantern still. I tried as steadily as I could to keep the ray of light upon the eye. All the while, the horrible

---

[5] **hideous**—horrible, ugly.

beating of the heart increased. It grew quicker and quicker, and louder and louder. The old man's terror must have been extreme! It grew louder, I say, louder every moment! Do you hear me? I have told you that I am nervous. Now, in the dead of night, this strange noise terrified me. Yet for some minutes longer I kept quiet. But the beating grew louder, louder! I thought the heart must burst.

But the beating grew louder, louder! I thought the heart must burst.

And now a new worry came upon me—the sound might be heard by a neighbor! So the old man's hour had come at last! With a loud yell, I threw open the lantern and jumped into the room. He shrieked once—once only. In an instant I dragged him to the floor and pulled the heavy bed over him. Then I smiled, because it had all been so easy! But, for many minutes more, the heart beat on with a muffled sound. This, however, did not trouble me; the sound could not be heard through the wall. At last, it stopped. The old man was dead. I removed the bed and examined the corpse. Yes, he was stone, stone dead. I placed my hand upon the heart and held it there many minutes. There was no pulse. He was stone dead. His vulture eye would bother me no more.

If you still think I'm crazy, you'll change your mind when I describe how well I hid the body. All through the night I worked in silence. First I cut off the head of the corpse, and then I cut off its arms and legs. Then I pulled up three floorboards and hid the body underneath. I then replaced the boards so carefully that no human eye—not even his!—could see that the boards had been moved. Ha! Ha! Is that the work of a madman?

I finished my work at close to four o'clock. It was still dark as midnight. As the clock chimed four, I heard a knocking at the door. I went down to open it with a light heart. What had I *now* to fear? I opened the door to three men, all of them police officers. A shriek had been heard by a neighbor during the night, they said. The officers had been sent to check the house.

I smiled—for *what* did I have to fear? I told the men they were welcome. The old man, I said, was on vacation in the country. I had shrieked in a dream. I took my visitors all over the house. I told them to search carefully. Eventually, I led them to the old man's bedroom. I showed them his treasures, which were completely safe and undisturbed. I was so confident, in fact, that I brought three chairs into the bedroom and asked the men to sit and rest. And then I—in a way that was perfectly calm, perfectly confident of my triumph—placed my own chair upon the very spot where I had hidden the dead body!

The officers were satisfied. My manner had convinced them. I was so calm! They sat and, while I answered cheerfully, they chatted about this and that. But before long, I felt myself growing pale and I wished they would go. My head ached, and I thought I heard a ringing in my ears. But still they sat and chatted. The ringing became more distinct—I heard it over the noise of their talk. I talked more freely so that I could not hear the noise, but it became louder and louder and louder. Eventually, I found that the noise was not in my ears at all.

No doubt, I had become very pale, but I talked more and more loudly. Yet the sound increased—and what could I do? It was a low, dull, quick sound, like the sound a watch makes when covered in cotton. I gasped for breath—and yet the officers did not hear it. I talked more quickly, but the noise steadily increased. I stood up and argued about silly things, using a high, loud voice and violent **gestures**,[6] but still the noise increased. Why didn't the officers leave? I paced the floor to and fro with heavy steps, but the noise got louder and louder. Oh, God! what could I do? I foamed at the mouth— I raved—I swore! I threw the chair upon which I had been sitting across the room, but the noise was everywhere! It grew louder—louder—louder! And still the men chatted pleasantly, and smiled. Was it possible they couldn't hear it? No, no! They heard! They suspected! They *knew*! They were silently laughing at my horror! This is what I thought then, and this is what I think now.

"Villains!" I shrieked. "Pretend no more! I admit the deed! Tear up the planks! Pull them up here and here! It is the beating of his hideous heart!"

THE END

---

[6] **gestures**—movements.

The Cask of Amontillado

Perhaps Poe's finest story, "The Cask of Amontillado"
(1846) takes place in Italy during the spring. The narrator,
Montresor, describes his plan of revenge on a "friend"
named Fortunato.

A thousand injuries from Fortunato I had **borne**[1] as
I best could, but when he insulted me, I could not
bear it. And so I vowed revenge.

You, who know me so well, will understand
that I never said anything about my revenge. There
was no need to say a word to anyone. I would have
my revenge eventually. I must not only punish

---

[1] **borne**—put up with.

him, but punish without being caught. And he must know that I was punishing him. In the meantime, I would wait, and I would plan to punish this man severely.

P lease understand that Fortunato never knew about my plan. For all he knew, I was his good friend. I smiled at him as I always had done. Only he did not know that I was smiling at the thought of his **destruction**.[2]

He had a weak point—this Fortunato—although in most ways he was a man people respected and even feared. But Fortunato was **vain**[3] about his knowledge of wine, old Italian wines in particular. And indeed, his knowledge was very, very good. In this respect, he and I were the same. I too have a great knowledge of Italian wines.

Early one evening, during the busy **carnival**[4] season, I began working my plan. I met Fortunato in the street in front of the **palazzo**.[5] He greeted me

---

[2] **destruction**—being destroyed, ruined.

[3] **vain**—overly proud.

[4] **carnival**—a time of feasting and merrymaking in Italy in the spring before Lent. During carnival, both children and adults wear costumes.

[5] **palazzo**—large, imposing building (such as a museum, palace, or house), especially in Italy.

warmly, for he had been drinking a great deal. Like the other men and women in the street, he wore a brightly-colored carnival costume, complete with a silly cap that was decorated with bells. I was so pleased to see him that I thought I would never finish shaking his hand.

> **"I've received a cask of what I've been told is Amontillado, but I have my doubts that it is real."**

I said to him, "My dear Fortunato, how lucky that we've run into each other like this! And how wonderful you look in your costume. But, Fortunato, I must have your advice. I've received a **cask**[6] of what I've been told is Amontillado,[7] but I have my doubts that it is real."

"What?" he asked. "A cask? Could you have received such a valuable shipment of wine, now, in the middle of carnival season?"

"I have my doubts," I replied, "and I was silly enough to pay the full Amontillado price without asking you first. You were nowhere to be found, and I was so afraid of losing a bargain."

"Amontillado!" he exclaimed again.

---

[6] **cask**—barrel.

[7] Amontillado—a medium dry sherry, which is a type of wine.

"I have my doubts," I said once more.

"Amontillado! Come, let us go."

"Where?" I asked, pretending confusion.

"To your wine cellar."

"My friend, no; I could not ask you to do such a thing. You are having such a great time at carnival—"

"I insist. Let's go."

"My friend, no. I am worried about the severe cold in my **vaults**,[8] which is where I've stored the cask. You'll catch a terrible cold."

"Let us go, nevertheless. The cold is nothing. A cask of Amontillado! Think of it!" With this, Fortunato grabbed hold of my arm and began pulling me along. I quickly pulled on a black silk mask and threw a carnival cape around my shoulders. Together, we made our way to my home.

My servants were not at home. I had told them that I'd be gone all night but they shouldn't leave the house, so they took that opportunity to sneak out to the carnival.

At the front of my house, several **torches**[9] glowed brightly. I pulled two off a wall and handed

---

[8] **vaults**—underground passages or rooms.

[9] **torches**—burning sticks of wood used to give light and usually carried in the hand.

one to Fortunato. He followed me through several rooms to the hallway that led to the vaults. Then we went down a long and winding staircase and came at last to the damp catacombs of the Montresors.[10]

Because he had been drinking, my friend's walk was unsteady, and the bells upon his cap jingled as he moved.

"The cask?" said he.

"It is farther on," said I. "But notice the damp that shines from these **cavern**[11] walls." He turned towards me and I gazed into his drunken eyes. "How long have you had that cough?" I asked.

"Ugh! ugh! ugh!—ugh! ugh! ugh!—ugh! ugh! ugh!—ugh! ugh! ugh!—ugh! ugh! ugh!" he coughed.

My poor friend couldn't answer for many minutes.

"It is nothing," he said, at last.

"Come," I said firmly, "we will go back; your health is precious. You are rich, respected, admired; you are happy, as once I was. You are a man to be

"You are rich, respected, admired; you are happy, as once I was. You are a man to be missed. For me it is no matter."

---

[10] catacombs of the Montresors—underground burial rooms in which the narrator's family was buried.

[11] **cavern**—cave.

missed. For me it is no matter. We must go back, or you will get sick. Besides, there is the carnival to think of—"

"Enough," he said. "The cough is nothing. It will not kill me. I will not die from a cough."

"True," I replied. "And I didn't mean to frighten you about your health. But you should be careful. A drink of this Medoc[12] will warm us."

Here I knocked the cork off a bottle which I drew from a long row of similar bottles. "Drink," I said, presenting him the wine.

He raised it to his lips with a **leer**.[13] He paused and nodded to me, while his bells jingled. "These vaults," he said, "are huge."

"The Montresors," I replied, "were a large and wealthy family."

"How true, how true. I'd forgotten that your family was once important." The wine sparkled in his eyes, and the bells on his hat jingled. My own face grew warm with the embarrassment from yet another insult. This man—he deserved all that I had planned for him!

We passed into the deepest regions of the catacombs. I paused again, and this time seized Fortunato by an arm above the elbow.

---

[12] Medoc—kind of red wine, from France.
[13] **leer**—sly smile.

"The damp!" I said. "We are below the river's bed. The drops of moisture are trickling upon our heads. Come, we will go back before it is too late. Your cough!"

"It is nothing," he said. "Let us go on. But first, another drink of the Medoc."

I handed him another bottle of wine, this one smaller. He emptied it in one breath. His eyes flashed with a fierce light. He laughed and threw the bottle upwards with a gesture I did not understand.

I looked at him in surprise. He repeated the movement—a **grotesque**[14] one.

"You do not understand?" he said.

"No," I replied.

"Then you are not of the brotherhood?"

"What brotherhood?"

"You are not of the Masons?"[15]

"Yes, yes," I said "Yes, I am."

"You? Impossible! A Mason?"

"Yes, a Mason," I replied.

"Give me a sign," he demanded.

"It is this," I answered, pulling a small shovel from underneath my cape.

---

[14] **grotesque**—odd or ugly; bizarre.

[15] Masons—worldwide secret society, whose purpose is mutual aid and fellowship. A mason (with a lowercase *m*) is someone who builds with stone or brick.

"You're joking," he exclaimed, moving away. "But let us proceed to the Amontillado."

"If you wish," I said, replacing the tool beneath the cape. Again I offered him my arm. He leaned upon it heavily. We continued in search of the Amontillado. We passed through a series of low arches and went further and further into the catacombs. The further we went, the dimmer our torches became. There was not enough air to feed the flames.

At the furthest end of the catacombs, there was a room that was smaller than all the others. Its walls had been lined by human remains piled as high as the ceiling.

At the furthest end of the catacombs, there was a room that was smaller than all the others. Its walls had been lined by human remains piled as high as the ceiling.

"Proceed," I said. "Straight ahead is the cask of Amontillado."

Fortunato stepped unsteadily forward, while I followed right at his heels. In an instant he had reached the far rock wall. There, he stood looking around, a confused expression on his face. Seeing my chance, I grabbed him. He was too surprised to resist. Working quickly, I threw two large chains around his waist and then locked the chains to two iron rods that had been bolted into the wall. After returning the key to my pocket, I stepped back to examine my work.

> Working quickly, I threw two large chains around his waist and then locked the chains to two iron rods that had been bolted into the wall.

"Pass your hand over the wall," I said. "Feel the damp. Indeed it is *very* damp. Once more let me *beg* you to return. No? Then I must positively leave you. But I must first make sure you are comfortable."

"The Amontillado!" moaned my friend, not yet recovered from his surprise.

"True," I replied, "the Amontillado."

As I said these words, I busied myself among the pile of bones that were lining the walls of the room. Throwing them aside, I soon uncovered a great deal of building stone and **mortar**.[16] Using these materials and my shovel, I began to wall up the entrance of the room.

I had scarcely laid the first layer of stone when I discovered that Fortunato was no longer drunk.

---

[16] **mortar**—type of cement.

The earliest sign I had of this was a low moaning cry from the back of the room. It was *not* the cry of a drunken man. There was then a long and stubborn silence. I laid the second layer of stone, and the third, and the fourth; and then I heard the furious rattling of the chains. The noise lasted for several minutes. During these minutes, I stopped what I was doing and sat down upon the bones so that I could listen to my prisoner's struggles. When the clanking ended, I picked up the shovel again and quickly built the fifth, the sixth, and the seventh layer. The wall was now nearly up to my chest. I paused again, this time to shine my weak torch at the man within.

A series of loud and shrill screams from the chained man made me take a step backwards. For a brief moment I hesitated—I trembled. Just as quickly, I calmed myself. I placed my hand on the solid stone of the catacombs and felt reassured. Once again, I began building my wall. Each time the chained figure yelled, I yelled louder. When he screamed, I screamed back. Eventually, my prisoner was silent.

It was now midnight, and my job was ending. I had completed the eighth, ninth, and tenth layers.

I had finished a portion of the final layer. There remained but a single stone to be fitted and plastered in. Now there came from the little room a low laugh that made the hairs on my neck stand on end. It was followed by a sad voice, which I had trouble recognizing as that of the **noble**[17] Fortunato. The voice said—

"Ha! ha! ha! He! he! A very good joke indeed—an excellent joke. We will have many laughs about it at the palazzo for months to come! He! He! He! He! We'll laugh about it over our wine!"

"Over our Amontillado!" I replied.

"He! he! he! Yes, the Amontillado. But isn't it getting late? Won't they be waiting for us at the palazzo, the Lady Fortunato[18] and the rest? Let us be gone."

"Yes," I said, "let us be gone."

"For the love of God, Montresor!"

"Yes," I said, "for the love of God!"

But to these words, there was no reply. I listened and waited and eventually grew impatient. I called aloud—

"Fortunato!"

No answer. I called again—

"Fortunato!"

---

[17] **noble**—grand. Montresor is being sarcastic.
[18] Lady Fortunato—Fortunato's wife.

No answer still. I thrust a torch through the hole in the wall and let it fall to the floor in the little room. In reply, there was only a jingling of the bells. My heart grew sick—on account of the dampness of the catacombs. I hurried to finish my work. I forced the last stone into its position and then plastered it up. Against the new wall I rebuilt the old wall of bones. For half of a century, no mortal has disturbed them. *Rest in peace.*

THE END

The Murders in the Rue Morgue

"The Murders in the Rue Morgue" (1841) is thought to be the first detective story ever published. In this mystery, the resourceful and intelligent C. Auguste Dupin and an unnamed friend (the narrator) help the police solve the horrible murders of two Parisian women.

Over the years, I have learned that the expression on a person's face can sometimes **contradict**[1] the words coming from the person's mouth. I am not alone in this observation. Some people take great pleasure in guessing exactly what another person's thoughts are, much to the astonishment of all present. These people

---

[1] **contradict**—be the opposite of.

love puzzles and games that involve mind-work. They *think* rather than *do* and are often thought of as lazy, even though quite the opposite is true.

But my purpose here is not to write a talk on the abilities of the mind. Rather, I am introducing my rather interesting story with a sort of rule that the reader should pay attention to: *To observe attentively is to remember **distinctly**.*[2] This said, I can now begin my story. The reader should keep my rule in mind.

While living in Paris during the spring and part of the summer of 18—, I became acquainted with Monsieur[3] C. Auguste Dupin. This young gentleman was of an excellent family that had recently fallen on some hard times. Dupin had become so poor that he lost his energy and became a kind of **recluse**,[4] who rarely left his house. Thanks to a small amount of money he had been given after a relative died, however, he was able to live comfortably on his remaining money, as long as he was very careful. His only luxury was books, and in Paris these are easy to get.

---

[2] **distinctly**—clearly.
[3] Monsieur—French word for *Mister*.
[4] **recluse**—person who has withdrawn from society.

We first met at a small library on the Rue[5] Montmartre. By chance, we were both searching for the very same book—a rare and unusual book that had been out of print for many years. We met over and over again, always searching for this same little book. Not surprisingly, we began to speak to one another. Dupin told me a little of his family history, which fascinated me. I was also astonished at the number of books he had read over the years. I told him that I was honored to meet such a knowledgeable man and that his company would do me a world of good. Eventually it was decided that I would stay with him while I was visiting Paris. Since I had more money than he did, it was agreed that I would rent a deserted, run-down old mansion on a quiet little street. I felt at home there almost immediately.

If our habits had been known to the world, people would have considered us madmen, though harmless. We lived completely alone and admitted no visitors. In fact, no one—not even my friends—knew where I lived. And, since Dupin had no real friends anymore, there was no chance that anyone would come to call. We existed within ourselves alone.

---

[5] Rue—French word for *street*.

My friend Dupin loved the night, and I soon learned to love it too. Because nights ended, we copied night during the day. At first light of dawn, we closed all the shutters of the house, lit a couple of sweet-smelling candles, and sat writing, talking, and reading the whole day. At the first sign of true darkness, we went out of the house and walked the streets, arm-in-arm, continuing our conversation among the wild lights and shadows of busy Paris. We looked for the mental excitement that results from quiet observation.

From the very start, I had noticed that Dupin had a quick and energetic mind. He had no friends and was very quiet, but he seemed to understand people well, and he often could tell what someone was thinking just by examining the expression on the person's face. He was, to be sure, a remarkably intelligent and **perceptive**[6] man.

Not long after I moved in with Dupin, we sat looking over an evening edition of the *Tribune Gazette.* We sat in silence, as was our habit, but we both read with interest the following paragraphs:

Extraordinary Murders—*This morning, about three o'clock, people living on the south side*

---

[6] **perceptive**—observant.

of Paris were awakened from sleep by a series of terrible shrieks that seemed to come from the fourth story of a house in the Rue Morgue. The house is owned by Madame[7] L'Espanaye and her daughter, Mademoiselle[8] Camille L'Espanaye.

Shortly after the screams began, a small group of neighbors, along with two police officers, gathered at the front of the house. After discovering that the front door to the house was locked, one of the police decided to break down the door with a **crowbar**.[9]

By the time the small group broke into the house, the screaming had stopped and all was silent. The group immediately rushed up the stairs, heading for the fourth floor. When they were close to the second landing, they heard two or more angry voices shouting at each other. By the time they reached the fourth landing, however, all was silent again. At this point, the group spread out and hurried from room to room. Eventually, several people arrived at a large back room on the fourth floor. Because the door was locked, with the key on the inside, the group had to waste several more moments forcing the door open.

---

[7] *Madame*—French word for *Mrs.*

[8] *Mademoiselle*—French word for *Miss.*

[9] **crowbar**—iron or steel bar, usually wedge-shaped at the working end, that is used to pry something up.

The room was in the wildest disorder—the furniture broken and thrown about in all directions. There was only one bed, and from this, the mattress had been removed and thrown into the middle of the floor. On a chair lay a razor, smeared with blood. On the **hearth**[10] were two or three long and thick **tresses**[11] of gray human hair (also dabbled with blood) that seemed to have been pulled out by the roots. On the floor was a hair comb, an earring, three large silver spoons, three smaller metal spoons, and two bags containing nearly four thousand francs[12] in gold. The drawers of a **bureau**,[13] which stood in one corner, were open. They looked as if someone had searched through them quickly and taken what they needed. A small iron safe was discovered under the mattress (not under the bed). It was open, with the key still in the door. There was nothing inside except for a few old letters and other papers of little interest.

A neighbor explained what happened next: "At first we could see no sign of Madame L'Espanaye. One member of our group noticed

---

[10] **hearth**—brick, stone, or cement area in front of a fireplace.

[11] **tresses**—long pieces of hair, or curls.

[12] francs—monetary unit of France.

[13] **bureau**—chest of drawers or desk.

an unusual amount of **soot**[14] in the fireplace, so he began to search the chimney. There he found (to our horror) the **corpse**[15] of the daughter, head downward. Four or five of us dragged her body from the chimney with some difficulty, as it had been forced up there quite a distance. The body was quite warm. Upon looking at it, many cuts and scratches were seen, no doubt caused by the rough bricks on the inside of the chimney. On the face were many severe scratches. Her throat, there were dark bruises and deep marks of fingernails, as if the girl had been **strangled**[16] to death."

After an investigation of the rest of the house, the group made its way into a small paved yard in the rear of the building. There they found the corpse of the old lady, with her throat entirely cut. In the attempt to pick her up off the ground, the head fell off. The body, as well as the head, was terribly bruised and battered—so much so that it was almost impossible to see the features of her face.

As of yet, the police have not a single clue as to who might have committed these horrible crimes.

---

[14] **soot**—black dust that is often found in a fireplace.

[15] **corpse**—dead body.

[16] **strangled**—choked.

The next day's paper had some additional information, which Dupin and I read with even more interest:

> **The Tragedy in the Rue Morgue**—*Many people have been questioned in relation to this frightful murder, but police are still puzzled as to what exactly happened on the fourth floor of the house on Rue Morgue.*
>
> *The **laundress**[17] for the house was a woman named Pauline Dubourg. She stated that she has known both of the **deceased**[18] for three years, having done washing for them during that period. They paid her well. The old lady and her daughter seemed to get along well and were very loving towards each other. Although Dubourg could not say for certain, she believed that Madame L. told **fortunes**[19] for a living. Dubourg also said she believed that the old woman had money put aside over the years. Dubourg was sure that the women had no servants in the house. There seemed to be no furniture in the house except on the fourth floor.*

---

[17] **laundress**—person who washes clothes.
[18] **deceased**—dead people.
[19] **fortunes**—predictions about a person's destiny or fate.

Pierre Moreau, tobacconist,[20] *said that he had been selling small quantities of tobacco to Madame L'Espanaye for nearly four years. According to Moreau, the deceased and her daughter had occupied the house on Rue Morgue for more than six years. Madame L. owned the house. The old woman was childish. Moreau had seen the daughter only five or six times over the last six years. The old lady and her daughter led very quiet lives and were said to have money put aside. Moreau had heard rumors that Madame L. told fortunes, but he did not believe it. He had never seen anyone enter the house except the old lady and her daughter, a handyman once or twice, and a doctor some eight or ten times.*

Many other neighbors said the same things. Most people were quick to point out that Madame L. and her daughter lived quiet lives. Some mentioned that the **shutters**[21] *of the front windows were hardly ever open. The shutters in the rear were always closed, with the exception of the large back room on the fourth floor. These shutters were usually open. The house itself was described as sturdy and in good condition.*

---

[20] *tobacconist*—one who sells cigars, cigarettes, and tobacco.

[21] **shutters**—moveable hinged screens or covers for a window.

Isidore Muset, police officer, said that he was called to the house about three o'clock in the morning. When he arrived, he found some twenty or thirty persons at the entrance trying to break down the door. Muset forced the door open with a **bayonet**[22]—not with a crowbar, as reported before. According to the officer, the screams continued until the door was forced open, and then they suddenly stopped. They seemed to be screams of some person (or persons) in great pain. They were loud and drawn out, not short and quick.

> They paused to listen to two angry voices that were clearly in the middle of an argument. The first voice was gruff; the second was high pitched and sounded strange.

Muset led the group upstairs. On reaching the second landing, they paused to listen to two angry voices that were clearly in the middle of an argument. The first voice was **gruff**;[23] the second was high pitched and sounded strange. It was not a woman's voice. Muset could make out a few words spoken by the gruff voice, which was that

---

[22] **bayonet**—blade attached to a rifle or other large gun that is used in hand-to-hand combat.

[23] **gruff**—rough-sounding.

of a Frenchman. He heard the words sacré[24] *and* diable.[25] *The shrill voice was that of a foreigner. Muset could not be sure whether it was the voice of a man or of a woman. Nor could he make out what was said, but he believed the person was speaking in Spanish.*

"Henri Duval, a neighbor, and by trade a silversmith,[26] said that he was among the first to enter the house. His information was essentially the same as that of Muset, although Duval mentioned that as soon as the group forced its way into the house they closed the front door in order to keep out the crowd that was gathering on the sidewalk. The shrill voice, Duval thinks, was that of an Italian. He did not know the Italian language, but was convinced that the speaker was speaking it. Duval knew Madame L. and her daughter. He had spoken with them frequently and was certain that the shrill voice was not that of either of the two women.

Monsieur Odenheimer, chef, volunteered information. Odenheimer, who is a native of Amsterdam, was examined through an interpreter,

---

[24] sacré—French word for *sacred* or for *damned*. The Frenchman was cursing.

[25] diable—French word for *devil*.

[26] *silversmith*—person who makes articles of silver.

since he speaks no French. This witness said that he was passing the house at the time of the shrieks. They lasted for several minutes—probably ten. They were long and loud—very awful and distressing. Odenheimer was among those who entered the house first. He agreed with all the other witnesses, but he said that he was certain that the shrill voice belonged to a man—a Frenchman. Odenheimer could not understand the words spoken, but said they were loud, quick, and "unequal." They were spoken in fear as well as in anger. He heard the gruff voice repeatedly say the words sacré, diable, *and* mon Dieu.[27]

Jules Mignaud, banker at Mignaud and Sons Bank, stated that Madame L'Espanaye had had an account at his bank for eight years. She made frequent deposits in small sums. She had not taken any money out of the account until three days before her death, when she took out the sum of 4,000 francs. This sum was paid in gold, and a bank clerk was sent with Madame L. to help her carry the money.

Adolphe Le Bon, a bank clerk, confirmed that he went with Madame L'Espanaye to her home with the 4,000 francs in two bags. When the

---

[27] mon Dieu—French words for *my God.*

front door was opened, Mademoiselle L. appeared and took one of the bags from him. The old lady took the other. Le Bon then bowed and left. He did not see anyone in the street at the time.

William Bird, a tailor and an Englishman, also gave **testimony**.[28] He entered the house along with Odenheimer and Duval and was one of the first to climb the stairs. Bird says that the gruff voice was most definitely that of a Frenchman. He too heard the words sacré and mon Dieu. He also heard what sounded like several persons struggling. The shrill voice was very loud. He thought that it was that of a German. It was definitely not an Englishman. Bird speaks no German.

Four of the witnesses stated that the door of the back room in which Mademoiselle L. was found was locked from the inside. When the group reached this door, they heard no groans or noises of any kind. When they forced the door open, they saw no one. The windows of both the back and front rooms were locked from the inside. A door between the two rooms was closed but not locked. The door leading from the front room into

---

[28] **testimony**—evidence, a sworn statement about the true facts as he understood them.

the hallway was locked, with the key on the inside. The door of a small room in the front of the house on the fourth floor was open. This room was filled with old beds, boxes, and so forth.

Every inch of the house has been searched by police in an attempt to find clues. Chimney-sweeping brushes were sent up and down the narrow chimneys. A trapdoor on the roof had been nailed down very securely. It did not appear to have been opened for years. The witnesses differed on the time between hearing arguing voices and breaking open the room door. Some said three minutes, and others said five.

Alfonzo Garcio, **undertaker**,[29] said that he was born in Spain. He was among the group that entered the house after hearing the screams. He was too nervous to climb the stairs, he said. He did hear the arguing voices, though, and said he was sure that the shrill voice belonged to an Englishman. Garcio speaks no English.

Alberto Montani, **confectioner**,[30] stated that he was one of the first to go up the stairs. He, too, heard the voices. The gruff voice, he said, was that of a Frenchman; the shrill voice was that of

---

[29] **undertaker**—someone who prepares the dead for burial.
[30] **confectioner**—someone who makes or sells candies and sweets.

a Russian. Montani, who is Italian, has never spoken with a native of Russia.

Several witnesses stated that the chimneys in the rooms on the fourth story were far too narrow for a human being to climb up. The body of Mademoiselle L'Espanaye was so firmly stuck in the chimney that it took the strength of four or five persons to pull her out. There is no back staircase, so the murderer could not have gone down while the group went up the stairs.

Paul Dumas, physician, stated that he was asked to view the bodies at around daybreak. At that point, both bodies were lying on the bed in the room where Mademoiselle L. was found. The corpse of the young lady was quite bruised and scratched. Dumas guessed that this happened when it was pushed up the chimney. The throat of the young woman was badly bruised. There were several deep scratches just below the chin, together with a series of marks that looked

> The body of Mademoiselle L'Espanaye was so firmly stuck in the chimney that it took the strength of four or five persons to pull her out.

exactly like the impression of fingers. The face was terribly discolored, and the eyeballs stuck out. The tongue had been partially bitten through. A large bruise was discovered upon the stomach, produced, apparently, by the pressure of a knee. In the opinion of M. Dumas, Mademoiselle L'Espanaye had been strangled to death by some person or persons unknown.

Dumas also reported that the corpse of the mother was horribly **mutilated**.[31] All the bones of the right leg and arm were shattered. The ribs on the left side were broken as well. The whole body was bruised and discolored. It was not possible to say how the injuries had been inflicted. A heavy wooden club or a large piece of furniture, such as a chair, would have produced such results if the blows were made by a very powerful man. Dumas believed that a woman could not have caused these injuries. The head of the deceased, which was entirely separated from the body, was also greatly shattered. The throat had evidently been cut with some very sharp instrument—perhaps a razor.

No other information of importance was given by witnesses, although police continue to

---

[31] **mutilated**—injured.

hold interviews. A murder so mysterious and so puzzling was never before committed in Paris—if indeed a murder has been committed at all. As of today, not the shadow of a clue has been found.

The evening edition of the paper stated that the greatest excitement continued to surround the Rue Morgue murders. The house had been carefully searched again, and all witnesses were questioned again. Still no clues were found. A note at the end of the paper, however, appeared about Adolphe Le Bon, the bank clerk who had helped the old lady home with her bags of gold. He had been arrested and imprisoned—although it seemed there was nothing to tie him to the crime.

Dupin was unusually interested in this crime, although he said very little about it. It was only after hearing that Le Bon had been imprisoned that he asked my opinion about the murders.

I told Dupin that I agreed with everyone in Paris that the crime would never be solved. It would be impossible to find the murderer.

"We must not reach that conclusion, just from what we have heard from the police," Dupin said with some energy. "The Parisian police are **cunning**,[32] but nothing else. They follow no plan other than the one described in their **manuals**.[33] For no reason will they change their ways to fit the nature of the crime. They are hard-working, but not imaginative.

"As for these murders, let us conduct an investigation ourselves before we form an opinion about them. We might find the effort amusing. And, besides, Le Bon once did me a favor, for which I am grateful.

Before going in, we walked up the street, turned down an alley, and then, again turning, went to the rear of the building.

We will go and see the house with our own eyes. I know G—, the chief of police. He will give us permission, I'm certain."

The next day, having received permission, we proceeded to the Rue Morgue. It was easy to spot the house, since many people were standing around staring up at it. Before going in, we walked up the street, turned down an alley, and then, again turning, went to the rear of the building. As we walked, Dupin examined the neighborhood and house very carefully.

---

[32] **cunning**—crafty.
[33] **manuals**—rulebooks.

Retracing our steps, we came again to the front of the house and rang the bell. A policeman answered and allowed us to enter. We went upstairs into the room where the body of Mademoiselle L'Espanaye had been found, and where both the deceased still lay. The room was in the same state the newspaper had described. Dupin inspected everything, even the bodies of the two women.

Next we went into the other rooms and into the yard. A policeman went with us everywhere. We stayed at the house the whole day, with Dupin inspecting every square inch. When it became too dark to see, we left the Rue Morgue and started back towards our house. On our way home, my companion stopped for a moment at the office of one of the daily newspapers.

Dupin did not discuss the murder until noon the next day. He then asked me, suddenly, if I had observed anything *peculiar* at the scene. Something about the way he said *peculiar* made me shiver.

"No, nothing peculiar," I said; "nothing more, at least, than what we both read in the paper."

"The *Gazette*," he replied, "may not have given us the whole story. Let us for a moment forget what the newspaper had to say.

"It appears to me that this mystery is considered impossible to solve for the very reason that should make it easy to solve. The police are confused because they lack a **motive**.[34] Interestingly, they are not confused by the motive for the murder itself but by the **atrocity**[35] of the murder.

"The police are also puzzled because witnesses heard voices coming from a room that was unoccupied, except for the body of the murdered Mademoiselle L'Espanaye. They are quite certain that the murderer could not have escaped the room without having been seen by the group on the stairs. So, they wonder, how did the murderer get out of the house? The police are blinded by the outward horror of the crime. They are stunned that the murderer pushed the corpse of the young girl's body up the chimney. They are also stunned by the frightful mutilation of the old lady's body. They have made the common error of assuming that because something is *unusual,* it is difficult to understand. In short, because they are puzzled, they have confused the unusual with the mysterious.

---

[34] **motive**—reason for acting.
[35] **atrocity**—excessive cruelty.

"In this type of investigation, however, it's important to ask not 'What has occurred?' but 'What has occurred that has never occurred before?' The police, who can only follow their manuals, are unable to ask this question."

I took the weapons, scarcely knowing what I did or believing what I heard.

I stared at Dupin, trying to decide what he meant by these words.

"I am now waiting," he continued, "for a person who, although perhaps not the murderer, is somehow involved in the crime. He probably was not in on the worst part of the crimes committed—namely, the murders. But make no mistake, he is involved in some of the events of that night.

"I look for the man here—in this room—every moment. It is true that he may not arrive; but I think he will. If he comes, it will be necessary to **detain**[36] him. Here are the guns. We both know how to use them if need be."

I took the weapons, scarcely knowing what I did or believing what I heard. Dupin ignored my confusion and went on speaking.

---

[36] **detain**—stop (from leaving).

"We know from the witnesses that the voices heard arguing," he said, "were not the voices of the women themselves. This lets us know that the old woman could not have first killed the daughter and afterward have committed suicide. Of this I am certain. Madame L'Espanaye was not strong enough to push her daughter's corpse up the chimney as it was found. Also, she could not have made the horrible wounds upon her own body. Murder, then, has been committed by some third party. I am convinced that it was the murderer or murderers that the witnesses heard arguing.

"Let us now discuss the witnesses' statements about the voices. I don't want to discuss all of the statements. Did you notice anything *peculiar* about the witnesses' recollections?"

I said that while all the witnesses agreed that the gruff voice had to belong to a Frenchman, there was much disagreement about the shrill voice.

"That was the evidence itself," said Dupin, "but you have not spoken of the *peculiarity* of the evidence. You have observed nothing special. Yet there *was* something to be observed. The witnesses, as you say, agreed about the gruff voice.

But in regard to the shrill voice, the peculiarity is not that they disagreed, but that each witness—an Italian, an Englishman, a Spaniard, a Dutchman, and a Frenchman—all insisted that the shrill voice was that of a foreigner. Each witness is sure that it was not the voice of one of his own countrymen. The Frenchman, who speaks no Spanish, says it was the voice of a Spaniard. The Dutchman says it had to have been that of a Frenchman, but we find that the man speaks no French. The Englishman thinks it the voice of a German, although he does not understand German. The Spaniard 'is sure' that the voice belonged to an Englishman, although he has no knowledge of English. The Italian believes it the voice of a Russian, but 'has never spoken with a native of Russia.' A second Frenchman is positive that the voice was that of an Italian, although he has no knowledge of Italian. Now think of it! How

But in regard to the shrill voice, the peculiarity is not that they disagreed, but that each witness—an Italian, an Englishman, a Spaniard, a Dutchman, and a Frenchman—all insisted that the shrill voice was that of a foreigner.

unusual—how *peculiar*—this voice must have been for it to have resulted in such testimony!

"Now let me call your attention to three points. The voice is described by one witness as 'harsh rather than shrill.' It is described by one or two witnesses as 'quick and unequal.' No words—no sounds resembling words—were heard by any of the witnesses.

"I don't know," he continued, "what impression I may have made so far upon your own understanding. But, I do know that it's possible to make intelligent **deductions**[37] about the voices that could be used to direct all further progress in the investigation.

"Let us leave the voices, for a moment, and think about the room on the fourth floor. The question here is how did the murderer exit the room without being seen? We know, of course, that Madame and Mademoiselle L'Espanaye were not murdered by ghosts. The murderers were human, and as such, needed an exit from the room. So let us examine each possible exit.

"It is clear that the murderer was in the room where Mademoiselle L'Espanaye was found. Or,

---

[37] **deductions**—inferences or reasonable guesses.

the very least was in the room next door, when the group of neighbors was climbing the stairs. The police have searched the floors, ceilings, and walls of these rooms. Not trusting them, I looked myself. There are no secret passageways. Both doors leading into the hallway were securely locked from the inside. The chimneys, although of an ordinary size in the lower part, are not wide enough to fit the body of a cat in the upper part. Therefore, we must rule out the chimneys. So all that is left are the windows. No one could have escaped through the windows of the front room, because the crowd on the street would have noticed. So the murderer must have left through the windows of the back room.

"There are two windows in the back room. One of them is not blocked and is wholly visible. The lower part of the other window is hidden from view by the **headboard**[38] of the heavy bed that is close up against it. The unblocked window was found securely fastened from the inside. No one could raise it. The other window was also found locked tight. It absolutely could not be opened, no matter how many men tried. A small hole had been made in the window frame to the left, and a very

---

[38] **headboard**—board at the head of a bed behind the pillow.

thick nail had been fitted into the hole. The nail was driven in so deep, in fact, that only the head was showing. Upon examining the other window, I found that it, too, had a thick nail that was driven deeply into the window frame. Because the windows were locked, and because the nails were in place in both windows, the police concluded that the murderer had not left the house by these windows. There was no need, they decided, to pull out the nails and open the windows.

> **"Yet the windows were locked. The windows then, must have the power of locking themselves."**

"My own examination of the windows was more thorough. I knew that the murderer or murderers *did* escape from these windows. This being so, they could not have locked the windows from the outside. Yet the windows were locked. The windows then, must have the power of locking themselves. There is no escaping this conclusion. I stepped to the window, took out the nail with some difficulty, and attempted to raise the window. It resisted all my efforts, as I had thought it would. I knew now that there must be a hidden **spring**[39] in this window. I could not yet explain the nails, but I knew that in a moment I would be able to explain the locks. A careful search soon brought to light the hidden spring. I pressed it and saw that the window now raised easily. When pressed again, the window slammed shut and locked.

"I now replaced the nail and looked at it carefully. Someone passing out through this window might have closed it after him, and the spring would have caught—but the nail could not have been replaced. The conclusion was plain. The murderers must have escaped through the other window. Supposing, then, that if the springs in each window are the same, as was probable, there must be a difference in the nails, or in the way the nails were hammered into the frame.

"By standing on the bed, I looked carefully over the headboard. Passing my hand down behind the board, I easily discovered and pressed the spring, which was, as I had supposed, the same as the one in the other window. I now looked at the nail. It was as thick as the other, and apparently fitted the hole in the exact same manner—driven in nearly up to the top.

---

[39] **spring**—coiled metal that jumps up when released.

"But I knew from my deductions that the two nails could not be exactly the same. 'There *must* be something wrong,' I said, 'with the nail.' I touched it, and the head, with about a quarter of an inch of the **shank**,[40] came off in my fingers. The rest of the shank was still in the hole, where it had been broken off. The break in the nail was an old one, since its edges were covered in rust. I now carefully replaced this head portion in the hole from which I had taken it, and once again, the nail looked completely whole. Pressing the spring, I gently raised the window a few inches. The head of the nail went up with it, although it remained in the hole. When I closed the window again, the head fell back into its normal position and looked whole again.

"The riddle, so far, was now solved. The murderer had escaped through the window that was partly blocked by the headboard. The window dropped of its own accord when the murderer

---

"But I knew from my deductions that the two nails could not be exactly the same. 'There must be something wrong,' I said, 'with the nail.'"

---

[40] **shank**—the long, straight piece underneath the head of the nail.

exited, and it once again became fastened by the spring. The police mistakenly thought that it was fastened by the nail.

"The next question concerns how the murderer got down from the fourth floor, once he was outside the window. This was easily enough determined. When you and I had walked around the building, I noticed that about five-and-a-half feet from the window there runs a lightning rod.[41] The murderer simply climbed down the shutters that hang on either side of the window. When he reached the bottom of the shutters, the murderer would have found himself within two feet of the lightning rod. At that point, he could have made a small jump onto the lightning rod and then climbed hand over hand down the rod.

"I wish you to notice now that what I am describing would have required a fair amount of skill on the part of the murderer. This man, I knew, would have to be unusually **agile**.[42]

"Next," he continued, "I shifted my focus from how the murderer got out to the murders

---

[41] lightning rod—rod fastened to the side and roof of a house that can attract lightning and ground the electric charge to protect the house from burning.
[42] **agile**—quick and nimble; able to move easily.

themselves. Think along with me, please. The drawers of the bureau, it is said, had been searched. Some items of clothing were thought to be stolen, although much clothing still remained. The conclusion that the murderer stole clothing is absurd. It is a mere guess—a very silly one—and no more. How are we to know that the articles found in the drawers were not all these drawers had originally contained? Madame L'Espanaye and her daughter lived a very lonely life. They had no company, and they did not often go out. So they had no use for many different outfits. The clothing found in the drawer was of an excellent quality. If a thief had taken some clothes, why didn't he take these as well? In fact, why did he leave 4,000 francs in gold only to load himself down with a bundle of clothes?

"This brings me to my next point, which has greatly puzzled the police. As you know, the gold was left behind. Nearly the whole sum mentioned by Monsieur Mignaud, the banker, was found in bags on the floor. Forget for a moment the police's idea that this is a robbery gone wrong. It is true that the old woman had recently taken out 4,000 francs from the bank. What I'd like to tell you, however, is that this money may be totally unrelated to the crime. Why else would the money have been left? If the money had been the motive, the murderer must have been an idiot to have left it. Clearly, robbery was not the motive here.

"Please continue to keep in mind the points I have already made—the odd voice, the unusual agility of the murderer, and the lack of a motive. Now let us glance at the murder itself. Here is a woman strangled to death and pushed up a chimney, head downward. The key here, of course, is the chimney. Why stuff the young lady up a chimney? This is something that an ordinary murderer would not bother to do. In fact, this is the act of a very sick person, someone who is mentally ill. Think, too, of how strong the murderer must have been to shove her body up so high into such a narrow space! Remember it took several persons to drag it back down!

Why stuff the young lady up a chimney? This is something that an ordinary murderer would not bother to do.

"On the hearth, underneath the chimney, were several clumps of gray human hair. These had been torn out by the roots. You are aware of the great force needed to tear clumps of hair from a human head. You saw the clumps yourself. Their roots (a terrible sight!) were clotted with fragments of the flesh of the scalp. The person who ripped these from the victim's head had to have had tremendous strength! Also remember that the throat of the old lady was not merely cut; the head was separated from the body. This act too shows a *brutal* strength, especially if it was indeed done with a razor. Madame L'Espanaye's body, as you'll recall, was badly bruised. Monsieur Dumas, the physician, said that the bruises were caused by a **blunt**[43] object, which seems correct. The blunt object, however, was clearly the stone pavement in the yard, upon which the victim had fallen. The old woman, I have figured out, was pushed or thrown out the window behind the bed. This idea, however simple it may now seem, escaped the police for the same reason that the shutters and lightening rod escaped them—because, thanks to the nails, they believed that the windows could not be opened.

"If now, in addition to all these things, you have thought about the odd mess in the room, the superhuman strength needed to pull clumps of hair out from the roots, and the horrible butchery done to these women without a motive, you will

---

[43] **blunt**—not sharp.

begin to have a more complete picture of who the murderer might have been. What impression do you have?"

I felt my flesh creep as Dupin asked me the question. "A madman," I said, "has done this terrible thing—some **raving**[44] madman, escaped from a neighboring hospital for the insane."

> *I felt my flesh creep as Dupin asked me the question. "A madman," I said, "has done this terrible thing."*

"In a way," he replied, "your idea is not a bad one. But the voices of madmen, even in their wildest moments, are not like the peculiar voice heard on the stairs. Besides, the hair of a madman is not what I hold in my hand now. I pulled this little **tuft**[45] from the fist of Madame L'Espanaye. Tell me what you can make of it."

"Dupin!" I said, completely astonished. "This hair is most unusual—this is not *human* hair."

"I have not said that it is," said he. "But before we decide this point, I wish you to glance at the little sketch I have traced on this paper. It is a drawing of what has been described in the testimony as 'dark

---

[44] **raving**—talking irrationally; not making any sense.
[45] **tuft**—bunch of hair.

bruises, and deep fingernail marks upon the throat of Mademoiselle L'Espanaye.'

"You will see," continued my friend, spreading out the paper upon the table before us, "that this drawing gives the idea of a firm and fixed hold. There is no sign that the murderer's hands slipped at all. Each finger has kept—possibly until the death of the victim—the fearful grasp that it started with. Now try to place all your fingers, at the same time, in the impressions you see here on the sketch."

I tried, but found it was impossible.

"We are possibly not giving this matter a fair trial," he said. "The paper is spread out upon a flat surface; but the human throat is curved. Here is a piece of wood, about the same size as a throat. Wrap the drawing around it and try the experiment again."

I did so, but the difficulty was even more obvious than before.

"This," I said, "is the mark of no human hand."

"You are correct. In fact, these finger marks could be made by no other mammal but an **orangutan**.[46] Only an orangutan could span a

---

[46] **orangutan**—large ape. The orangutan is about two-thirds as large as the gorilla and has brown skin, long reddish-brown hair, and very long arms.

woman's throat like this. Only an orangutan could have such incredible strength and be so fierce."

At this point, Dupin handed me a book of mammals. "I see here," I said, looking at a drawing, "that the tuft of hair that you hold in your hand matches exactly the color and texture of the hair of an orangutan. But Dupin, I cannot understand this frightful mystery. How could an orangutan have gotten into the house? And have you forgotten? There were two voices heard in argument, and one of them was unquestionably the voice of a Frenchman."

"True, and you will also remember that the Frenchman at one point was heard to say, '*mon Dieu*!' with some **dismay**.[47] Upon these two words, therefore, I have mainly built my hopes of a full solution to the mystery. A Frenchman saw the murder. It is possible—in fact it is more than probable—that he did not take part in the bloodshed. Perhaps the orangutan escaped from him. Perhaps the Frenchman *owns* the orangutan. He may have followed it to the house and been unable to recapture it. If that is the case, then the animal is still roaming Paris

---

[47] **dismay**—horror.

somewhere. I am not sure of this, of course. I am simply guessing. But if the Frenchman in question is, indeed, innocent of the murders, then this ad which I left last night in the newspaper office on our way home, will bring him to our house."

He handed me a paper, and I read the ad he had placed:

Caught—*In the south of Paris, a very large orangutan of the Bornese[48] species. The owner, who may be a sailor belonging to a Maltese[49] ship, may have the animal again, upon identifying it satisfactorily and paying a few charges arising from its capture and keeping. Call on M. Dupin, No.— , Rue—, Paris.*

"How is it possible," I asked, "that you know the man is a sailor, and belonging to a Maltese ship?"

"I do *not* know it," said Dupin. "I am not *sure* of it. Beneath the lightning rod, I found a piece of greasy ribbon that Maltese men use to tie back their hair. The knot is one that only sailors can tie.

"If I am right, the sailor will see this advertisement and wonder if it is safe to come get

---

[48] *Bornese*—of or relating to Borneo, a large island in the South China Sea.
[49] *Maltese*—from Malta, an island in the Mediterranean Sea.

the orangutan. He will take the chance, I believe, because the orangutan is a very valuable animal. Also, he will think he is safe because the police clearly have found no clues to link his animal to the crime scene at the Rue Morgue."

At this moment, we heard a step upon the stairs.

"Be ready," said Dupin, "with your pistols. But don't use them or show them until you have a signal from me."

The front door of the house had been left open, and the visitor had entered without ringing. First he climbed several steps upon the staircase. Now, however, he stopped for a moment, as if unsure what to do. Soon we heard him going down the stairs. Dupin was moving quickly to the door when we heard him coming up again. He did not turn back a second time, but stepped up with decision and rapped at the door of our room.

"Come in," said Dupin, in a cheerful and hearty tone.

A man entered. He was a sailor, as Dupin had predicted. He was a tall, stout, and muscular-looking person, with a certain daredevil expression on his face. He had with him a huge wooden club, but appeared to be otherwise unarmed. He bowed awkwardly and said "good evening" with a French accent.

"Sit down, my friend," said Dupin. "I suppose you have come about the orangutan. I must say, I almost envy you the possession of him. He is clearly a fine and very valuable animal. How old do you think he is?"

The sailor took a long, relieved breath and replied:

"I have no way of telling—but he can't be more than four or five years old. Have you got him here?"

"Oh no, we could not keep him here. He is at a stable nearby. You can get him in the morning. Of course, you are prepared to identify him as yours?"

"To be sure I am, sir."

"I shall be sorry to part with him," said Dupin.

"I don't mean that you should be at all this trouble for nothing, sir," said the man. "I wouldn't expect it. I am very willing to pay a reward for the finding of the animal—that is to say, anything in reason."

"Well," replied my friend, "that is all very fair, to be sure. Let me think!—what should I have? Oh! I will tell you. My reward shall be this. You shall give me all the information in your power about those murders in the Rue Morgue."

Dupin said the last words in a very low tone, and very quietly. Just as quietly, too, he walked toward the door, locked it, and put the key in his pocket. He then drew a pistol from his pocket and placed it quietly upon the table.

He jumped to his feet and grabbed his club, but the next moment he fell back into his seat, trembling violently, his face as pale as death.

The sailor's face turned bright red. He jumped to his feet and grabbed his club, but the next moment he fell back into his seat, trembling violently, his face as pale as death.

"My friend," said Dupin, in a kind tone, "you are alarming yourself unnecessarily—you are indeed. We mean you no harm. I promise that we plan no injury. I know that you are innocent of the murders in the Rue Morgue. It will not do, however, to deny that you are in some way involved. You have nothing to hide. On the other hand, you are bound by every principle of honor to confess all you know. An innocent man is now in prison, charged with the crime of murder."

The sailor recovered a bit while Dupin talked, but his original boldness was gone.

"So help me God," said he, after a brief pause, "I will tell you all I know, but I do not expect you to believe one-half of what I say. Still, I am innocent, and I will tell you everything."

What he told us was this. He had lately made a voyage to the East Indies. He was part of a group that landed at Borneo. He and another man captured the orangutan while in the jungle. Later, when his friend died unexpectedly, the orangutan fell into the sailor's care. After great trouble, which was made worse by the **ferocious**[50] nature of the animal, he eventually succeeded in bringing it to Paris. He hid it in his own house. His plan was to sell the animal once it had recovered from a wound in its foot.

Returning home from a bar one night, however, he found the orangutan in his own bedroom. The animal had broken out of the closet where it had been chained. A razor in hand, and fully **lathered**,[51] the orangutan was sitting in front of the mirror, trying to shave. It had undoubtedly watched its master do the same. Terrified at the sight of such a dangerous weapon in the hands of such a ferocious

---

[50] **ferocious**—very fierce.

[51] **lathered**—foamed up, as if with shaving cream.

animal, the man did not know what to do. He had been used to using a whip to quiet the animal. This always had worked in the past. The sailor pulled out the whip and headed towards the orangutan. When the orangutan saw the whip, it ran with great speed out the open door of the house and into the street.

The Frenchman followed as quickly as he could. The ape, razor still in hand, occasionally stopped to look back and then kept on running. The chase continued for a long time. Because it was three o'clock in the morning, no one saw what was happening. Eventually the ape found an alley at the rear of the Rue Morgue. It saw an open window on the fourth floor of a building and immediately began climbing the lightning rod towards the window. Then it climbed up the shutters of a back window and swung onto the headboard of the bed through the open window.

The sailor, in the meantime, was both relieved and confused. He had strong hopes now of capturing the animal. It could hardly escape from the building it had just entered. On the other hand, he was anxious about what it might do in the house. Because of this, the man decided to follow the animal. Without difficulty, the sailor climbed the lightning rod. At the top, however, he found himself unable to reach the shutter. All he could do was catch a glimpse of what was happening inside the house. When he looked in the window, he nearly fell from the rod—what he saw was so terrible. At this point, the terrible screams from inside the Rue Morgue began.

As the sailor watched, the gigantic animal seized Madame L'Espanaye by the hair (which was loose, as she had been combing it), and began waving the razor about her face, in imitation of the motions of a barber. The daughter lay still on the floor. She had fainted. The screams and struggles of the old lady (during which the hair was torn from her head) had the effect of making the orangutan angry. With one determined sweep of its muscular arm, it nearly cut her head from her body. The sight of blood made the orangutan even angrier. Grinding its teeth and flashing fire from its eyes, it flew upon the body of the girl and sunk its strong fingers into her throat, holding on tightly until she died.

Immediately after the young girl's body went limp, the orangutan caught sight of its master staring in horror through the window. The ape, no doubt, was still thinking about the dreaded whip. Its anger changed into fear. Knowing that it had done wrong, the animal began racing around the room in a highly nervous state. It threw down and broke furniture as it moved, and it dragged the mattress from the frame. Finally, it seized the body of the daughter and pushed it up the chimney. Then it seized the corpse of the old lady and threw it out the open window. The sailor guessed that the ape may have been trying to hide what it had done, like a small child tries to hide his or her mistakes.

As the ape approached the window with the corpse of the old woman, the sailor shrank back against the rod. He slid down it and decided to run for his life. He did not want to be involved in the murder and certainly wanted nothing more to do with the orangutan. The words heard by the group on the staircase were the Frenchman's shouts of horror, along with the devilish jabberings of the animal.

I have almost nothing left to tell. The orangutan must have escaped from the chamber, by the rod, just before the group broke down the door. It must have closed the window as it passed through it. The owner caught the orangutan later near a zoo in the center of Paris. Le Bon was released after we told G— and the other policemen the strange story. G—, although happy to have the crime solved, was embarrassed by his mistakes and made a few quiet comments to Dupin about people minding their own business.

"Let them talk," said Dupin, who had not thought it necessary to reply to G—. "Let G— talk about me and my methods. It will ease his conscience. For myself, I am satisfied with having defeated him in his own castle."

THE END

The Purloined Letter

In "The Purloined Letter" (1844) C. Auguste Dupin, Police Chief G——, and the unnamed narrator once again try to solve the puzzle of the "perfect" crime.

In Paris, just after dark one windy evening in the autumn of 18——, I was relaxing with my friend, C. Auguste Dupin, in his house at 33 Rue[1] Dunot, in the St. Germain district of Paris. For at least one hour we had been totally quiet. We were both staring at the smoke of our pipes. We were keeping our thoughts to ourselves, which is what Dupin usually preferred. For my part, I was thinking about a case that had recently interested me: the

---

[1] Rue—French word for *street.*

murders at the Rue Morgue. It seemed to be a **coincidence**,[2] therefore, when in walked another old friend, Monsieur[3] G—, the Paris Chief of Police.

Dupin and I gave him a hearty welcome, since we had not seen him for several months. Almost immediately, G— told us that he came on official business. He had a problem he wished to discuss with us.

"Then let us listen to your problem in the dark," said Dupin. "We can think more clearly if there is no light."

"That is another of your odd opinions," said the chief. He liked to use the word *odd* if he didn't quite understand something and therefore lived among a thousand "oddities."

"Very true," said Dupin, as he gave his visitor a pipe and invited him to sit in a comfortable chair.

"And what is the problem now?" I asked. "Not another murder, I hope?"

"Oh, no, nothing like that," he replied. "I've come with a very simple problem—one that I'm sure we can solve. I thought Dupin would like to hear the details because the problem is a very odd one."

"Simple and odd," said Dupin.

---

[2] **coincidence**—when two things happen at the same time, possibly by chance.
[3] Monsieur—French word for *Mister*.

"Well, yes, but not exactly that, either," G— said with some hesitation. "The fact is, we have been very puzzled, because the case *is* so simple."

"Maybe it's the simplicity of the case that confuses you," suggested Dupin.

"What nonsense!" replied the chief, laughing heartily.

"Maybe the mystery is a little too simple, a little too self-evident," said Dupin again.

"Ha! ha! ha! Ho! ho! ho!" roared the chief. "Oh, Dupin, who ever heard of such an idea?"

"But what, after all, is the case that's bothering you?" I asked.

"Why, I will tell you," replied the chief, as he settled himself in his chair. "I will tell you in a few words. But, before I begin, let me warn you that this is a secret matter. I could lose my job if this got out."

"We understand," I said. "Proceed."

"Or don't," said Dupin. "It's your case, after all."

"Well, then, I have received information from a very good source that a certain important document has been **purloined**[4] from the royal family. The

---

[4] **purloined**—stolen.

person who purloined it is known. He was seen taking it. It is also known that he still has the letter."

"How is this known?" asked Dupin.

"We know this because if the person who purloined the letter had sold it, or given it away, we would most definitely have heard about it."

"Please explain," I said.

"Well, I must tell you that the letter gives the person who holds it some power over the royal family," replied the chief.

"Still, I do not quite understand," said Dupin.

"No? Well, the letter contains information that could forever damage the career of a politician—and his wife—both of whom shall remain nameless."

"But the one who purloined the letter—how could he or she be so bold as to have admitted taking the letter?" I asked.

"The thief," said G—, "is the Minister D—. As you know, Minister D— is a **ruthless**[5] man. He is both bold and clever and will stop at nothing to advance his career. The letter was originally received by the royal person while she was alone in her sitting room. As she was reading it, she

---

[5] **ruthless**—without pity or compassion.

suddenly was interrupted by another person, her husband. The lady in question—not wanting to be seen with the letter—quickly put it down upon a table.

"After another moment or two, the Minister D— came to call. He entered the room, immediately spotted the letter, and recognized the handwriting. Undoubtedly, he also saw how nervous the lady was. Without a word, he pulled from his own pocket a letter that looked somewhat similar to the first. He opened his letter, pretended to read it, and then put it on the table next to the first letter. Then he sat and spoke about politics for perhaps fifteen minutes.

Eventually, as he said good-bye, he picked up the letter that was not his and put it in his pocket. The owner of the letter saw this but, of course, said nothing. She did not want her husband to know she had received this letter. The minister, after putting the stolen letter in his pocket, said good-bye and then left. Since then, he has been threatening to reveal the contents of the letter. In other words, he is using the letter to gain power and is **blackmailing**[6] the letter's owner."

---

[6] **blackmailing**—asking for money or other benefits from someone in exchange for not revealing something that might damage that person's reputation.

"I believe I understand the situation," said Dupin to me.

"Yes," replied the chief. "The person who was robbed is desperate to have the letter returned. This is why she called me and begged me to help."

"Than whom," said Dupin with a straight face, "no more intelligent agent can be found."

"You **flatter**[7] me," replied the chief; "but it is possible that she has this opinion of me."

"It is clear," I said, "that this Minister D— still holds the letter. Otherwise, the blackmailing could not continue."

"This is true," said G—. "My first step was to search the minister's house. I did so in secret, as I did not want him to know that the police had been called in on the matter."

"But the Parisian police have often done such things before?" I asked.

"Yes," said G—. "As you know, I have keys that can open any door in Paris. For three months, I have been searching the minister's rooms in secret, while he was out. I am determined to solve this crime myself, as my pride is at stake. Also, I must admit, there is a very large reward for the person who finds the letter. I searched every corner of that house, but I could find nothing. I did not stop

---

[7] **flatter**—praise too much.

searching until I was sure that the thief is more clever than I am."

"Isn't it possible," I suggested, "that the minister hid the letter elsewhere—outside of his house?"

"I suppose it is possible," said G—. "But I think D— is keeping it at his house, so that he can get his hands on it at a moment's notice. This would be a part of his plan, I am guessing."

"Perhaps he keeps it in his pocket at all times?" I asked.

"We know he does not," said the chief. "He has been searched twice now on his routine visits to the palace. No letter has been found."

"You might have saved yourself the trouble," said Dupin. "D— is clearly no fool. He would expect to be searched sooner or later."

"Well, perhaps he is not a *complete* fool," G— said reluctantly. "But he is a poet, which means he is at least partly a fool."

"True," said Dupin, after a long puff on his pipe, "although I have been guilty of writing some poor poetry myself."[8]

---

[8] Poe was proud of his own poetry.

"Suppose you give us details," said I, "about the search you made of his house."

"Why, the fact is, we took our time, and we searched everywhere," the chief explained. "I have a long experience of detective work. I took the entire building, room by room, and spent an entire week on the search. First we examined the furniture in each room. We opened every possible drawer. As I'm sure you know, to a properly trained police officer, there is no such thing as a secret drawer. After searching every cabinet, we searched every chair. We probed the cushions with fine, long needles. Then we took the tops off all the tables to check that a secret space did not exist inside the legs of the table. We did the same with all the bedposts.

"Next we used a powerful magnifying glass to examine the joints of every piece of furniture. If the joint had been recently glued, or disturbed in any way, we would have detected it. A single wood shaving, for example, would have been as obvious as an apple."

"I assume you looked at the mirrors, between the boards and the plates, and you looked through the beds and the blankets, as well as the curtains and carpets," I remarked.

"Yes, of course we did. And when we were satisfied that we had searched every piece of furniture, we began to examine the house itself. We used the magnifying glass to look at every square inch of that house, and the two houses on either side."

"The two houses next door!" I exclaimed. "You must have had a great deal of trouble."

"Yes, but the reward offered is huge," replied the chief quietly.

"You searched the **grounds**[9] of the houses?"

"All the grounds are paved with brick. They gave us very little trouble. We examined the **moss**[10] between the bricks, and found it undisturbed."

"You looked at D—'s papers, of course, and into the books of the library?"

"Certainly. We opened every package and parcel. We opened every book, turned over each page, checked every spine, and checked every book cover with the magnifying glass."

"Did you explore the floors beneath the carpets?" I asked.

"Absolutely. We removed every carpet and examined the boards with the magnifying glass."

"And the wallpaper on the walls?"

"Yes."

---

[9] **grounds**—property, land.
[10] **moss**—clumps of tiny plants that grow where it's damp or dark.

"You looked in the basement?"

"We did."

"Then," I said, "I believe you have been mistaken all along. The letter is not in D—'s house."

"I fear you are right there," said the chief. "And now, Dupin, what would you advise me to do?"

"I'd like you to search again," Dupin replied again with a small smile.

"That is absolutely unnecessary," replied G—. "I am certain the letter is not there."

"I have no better advice to give you," said Dupin. "You have, of course, an accurate description of the letter?"

"Oh yes!" said the chief, pulling out a notebook. He then read to us a thorough description of the appearance of the missing letter. He also read to us a summary of the letter's contents. After that, he left us to think about the puzzle.

About a month afterwards, G— paid us another visit, and found us again in Dupin's study, smoking. He took a pipe and a chair and began chatting about everyday matters. Finally, I interrupted him and said—

"Well, but G—, what of the purloined letter? Did you re-examine the minister's home?"

"**Confound**[11] him, yes. We searched the house again, just as Dupin suggested we do, but it was a waste of time. The letter is not there."

"How much was the reward offered, did you say?" asked Dupin.

"Why, it is very large. I don't want to say how large, exactly, but I will say that I will give the person who could get me the letter a reward of fifty thousand **francs**.[12]

"The fact is, the royal person who has offered the reward is becoming more and more desperate. She has just today said that she would double the reward. Still, it doesn't matter. I've tried and tried, and I cannot find that letter."

"Well, yes," said Dupin, slowly, between the puffs from his pipe. "I really think, G——, that there is more that you could do."

"Like what, for example?"

"Why—*puff, puff*—you might—*puff, puff*—find an advisor of some type—*puff, puff, puff.* But would you be willing to pay such an advisor and take his advice?"

"Well," said G——, a little uncomfortable, "I am perfectly willing to take advice and to pay for it. I would really give fifty thousand francs to anyone who would help me in the matter."

---

[11] **Confound**—darn.

[12] **francs**—monetary unit of France.

"In that case," replied Dupin, opening a drawer, and producing a checkbook, "you may as well write a check out for the amount mentioned. When you have signed it, I will hand you the letter."

I was astounded, and G— seemed to be absolutely **thunderstruck**.[13] For a few minutes, he sat without speaking or moving. He simply stared at Dupin with his mouth open wide. Then, without a word, he grabbed the pen, made out a check for fifty thousand francs, and handed it to Dupin. Dupin examined it carefully and then placed it in his wallet. Then he walked to his desk, unlocked a drawer, took out a letter, and handed it to the chief.

For a few minutes, he sat without speaking or moving. He simply stared at Dupin with his mouth open wide.

Chief G— grasped the letter with joy, opened it carefully, and reviewed its contents. Then, after scrambling to his feet, he rushed out the door, clutching the letter to his chest. He hadn't said a word since Dupin had asked him to fill out the check.

When he had gone, my friend decided to explain.

---

[13] **thunderstruck**—amazed.

"The Parisian police," he said, "are very skillful in their own way. They are **persevering**,[14] thorough, and knowledgeable about their duties. So, when G— told us about his search methods, I felt certain that he had made a satisfactory investigation, *so far as his labors[15] extended.*"

"So far as his labors extended?" said I.

"Yes," said Dupin. "His search was thorough. If the letter had been anywhere hidden in that house, the police would have found it.

"But as usual," Dupin continued, "the chief has made the common error of being either too deep or too shallow. He was too deep in his examination of the house, and too shallow in his examination of the man."

"I'm afraid I don't understand," I said.

"You recall that on Chief G—'s first visit, he called D— a fool?"

"Yes. I remember that he said that the minister is at least partly a fool, since he is a poet, and all poets are fools. But I fail to see how that relates. The minister, as you know, is a mathematician, not a poet."

"You are mistaken. I know the man well; he is both. And because he is both a poet and mathematician, he

---

[14] **persevering**—persistent, following a course of action in spite of difficulties.
[15] *labors*—work.

is able to **reason**.[16] If he were a mathematician alone, he would be unable to reason and would have been captured long ago by the chief."

"You surprise me with these opinions," I interrupted. "Mathematicians are known for their ability to reason."

"I'm afraid I must correct you. Mathematicians feel they can reason, but they are sadly mistaken. Their thinking is **linear**,[17] and they cannot think outside of a set formula. In fact, mathematicians are very much like police officers.

"If D— were a mathematician alone, then he would have thought about this letter in an entirely **predictable**[18] way. In fact, he would have done exactly what the chief expected him to do—that is, hide the letter in a predictable place, such as under the carpet or in a hole carved out of a bedpost.

"But, since D— is also a poet, he was able to think about things more creatively. He must have known that the first step of the police would be to give his house a thorough search. He also must have known that he himself also would be thoroughly searched.

---

[16] **reason**—draw conclusions in a systematic, thoughtful way.

[17] **linear**—in a straight line, with no deviation.

[18] **predictable**—able to be told beforehand.

"The chief told us that D— 'conveniently' left his house every night. I suggest that D— did this in order to give the police a chance to make their search. D— knew that they would eventually come up empty-handed. He assumed (and his assumption proved correct, as you and I know) that the police would finally decide that the letter was not in the house."

I listened carefully to Dupin's explanation, but remained confused.

"Do you remember how that first night, when I suggested that the reason the mystery troubled G— so much was because it was so simple?"

"Yes," said I, "I remember his laughter well."

"Well, my friend, it turns out that the joke is on the chief. The minister, knowing that the police search would be thorough to the last degree, decided to hide the letter in *plain sight*. He left the letter in plain sight, knowing that the police would ignore what was in plain sight and spend their time looking for something that was hidden.

"Knowing that the letter would be in plain sight, for all the world to see, I came up with a quick plan. The morning after our visit from the chief, I put a pair of green sunglasses in my pocket and walked over to D—'s home. I found D— at home lying around and pretending to be thoroughly bored.

"To be even with him, I put on my green sunglasses, explaining that I had weak eyes. Then, under cover of the glasses, I carefully and thoroughly checked the room. My host—who could not see my eyes—assumed that I was staring straight at him.

"I paid special attention to a large desk near which D— sat. On the desk lay a few letters and papers, with one or two musical instruments and a few books. I stared at the papers for a bit, but then decided there was nothing there of any interest.

"Next my eyes fell upon a card-rack that hung dangling from a dirty blue ribbon beneath the **mantelpiece**.[19] Inside the card-rack were three or four slots that held several visiting cards and a **solitary**[20] letter. The letter, I noticed, was very dirty and crumpled. It was torn nearly in two, across the middle, as if someone had decided it was worthless and was considering throwing it away. The letter had a large black seal and was addressed, in a dainty female hand to D—, the minister himself. The letter had been put carelessly into the top of the rack.

"I knew in a moment that this was the letter I was searching for. To be sure, it looked very different from the letter the chief had described. But the fact that the letter was so torn and dirty was a clue. The minister,

---

[19] **mantelpiece**—shelf above a fireplace.

[20] **solitary**—single.

I knew, would never have such a messy document lying around. Also, the size of the letter was exactly the size that G— had described. Plus—and this was my most important clue—the letter was *in plain sight*.

> **While I kept D—'s attention by discussing matters that I knew would interest him, I studied the letter.**

"I stayed at the minister's house as long as I could. While I kept D—'s attention by discussing matters that I knew would interest him, I studied the letter. I memorized its appearance and where it sat in the rack. The more I looked at the letter, the more convinced I became. The folds of the paper looked as if they had been folded once and then folded again, so that the inside section was now on the outside. I guessed that D— had simply turned the original letter to its blank side, written a phony address, and then resealed the letter.

"Without further delay, I said good-bye to the minister. Before I went, however, I left my gold **snuffbox**[21] upon the table.

"The next morning I called for the snuffbox. The minister and I continued our conversation of the

---

[21] **snuffbox**—box that holds snuff, a powdery tobacco that is taken up the nose.

previous day. After a moment or two, we heard the sharp sound of a gun being fired. Then there was a series of terrible screams. D— rushed to the window, threw it open, and looked out. In the meantime, I stepped to the card-rack, took the letter, put it in my pocket, and replaced it with a copy that I had carefully prepared beforehand. I made the outside of my letter look torn and dirty, just like the original.

"The noise in the street had been caused by a man with a rifle. He had fired it among a crowd of women and children. The gun wasn't loaded, however, so after things quieted down, he was able to slip away. When he had gone, D— came away from the window, where I had followed him as soon as I switched the letters. The man with the rifle was someone I had hired for the job."

"But why did you replace the letter with a copy?" I asked. "Wouldn't it have been better, on the first visit, to simply have grabbed the letter and left?"

"D—," replied Dupin, "is a desperate and brave man. His house, too, is filled with servants who would have done whatever he asked. Had I made this wild attempt, as you suggest, I might never have left the house alive. Also, I had the royal lady to think of. For eighteen months, D— has had her in his power. Now that she has the letter back, he is in *her* power. The next time he tries to blackmail her, she will have him arrested."

I chuckled at his reasoning. "What about the letter that you left? Did you write anything in that?"

"Well, it didn't seem right to leave it blank. Since D— once insulted me in Vienna many years ago, I thought this might be an excellent chance to repay him. I decided to leave him a clue about the identity of the person who took the letter. He knows my writing, so I simply wrote my initials— C.A.D.—in the middle of the blank page."

THE END

Annabel Lee

*In "Annabel Lee" (1849), Poe explores one of his favorite
poetic themes: the death of a beautiful young girl. The
narrator of the poem is Annabel Lee's husband. He is
grieving because his beautiful young bride is lost to
him forever.*

It was many and many a year ago,
    In a kingdom by the sea
That a maiden there lived whom you may know
    By the name of ANNABEL LEE;
And this maiden she lived with no other thought
    Than to love and be loved by me.

I was a child and *she* was a child,
In this kingdom by the sea;
But we loved with a love that was more than love—
      I and my ANNABEL LEE—
With a love that the winged seraphs[1] of heaven
      Coveted[2] her and me.

And this was the reason that, long ago,
      In this kingdom by the sea,
A wind blew out of a cloud, chilling
      My beautiful ANNABEL LEE;
So that her highborn kinsmen[3] came
      And bore her away from me,
To shut her up in a sepulcher[4]
      In this kingdom by the sea.

The angels, not half so happy in heaven,
      Went envying her and me—
Yes!—that was the reason (as all men know,
      In this kingdom by the sea)
That the wind came out of the cloud by night,
      Chilling and killing my ANNABEL LEE.

---

[1] seraphs—angels.

[2] Coveted—wanted to have very badly; were jealous of.

[3] highborn kinsmen—upper-class relatives.

[4] sepulcher—burial place; tomb.

But our love it was stronger by far than the love
    Of those who were older than we—
    Of many far wiser than we—
And neither the angels in heaven above,
    Nor the demons[5] down under the sea,
Can ever dissever[6] my soul from the soul
    Of the beautiful ANNABEL LEE:

For the moon never beams, without bringing me
                    dreams
    Of the beautiful ANNABEL LEE;
And the stars never rise, but I see the bright eyes
    Of the beautiful ANNABEL LEE:
And so, all the night tide, I lie down by the side
Of my darling—my darling—my life and my bride,
    In her sepulcher there by the sea—
    In her tomb by the sounding[7] sea.

---

[5] demons—evil spirits.

[6] dissever—separate.

[7] sounding—making a full, deep sound (as from the waves).

To Helen

"To Helen" (1831) celebrates the loveliness of one woman in particular and the beauty of all women in general. The Helen of the title is Helen of the ancient Greek city-state Troy. Her kidnapping caused the Trojan War. She was called the most beautiful woman of all time. This poem was addressed to the mother of one of Poe's school friends, who had died young.

Helen, thy[1] beauty is to me
    Like those Nicéan barks of yore,[2]
That gently, o'er[3] a perfumed sea,
    The weary, way-worn wanderer bore
    To his own native shore.

---

[1] thy—your.
[2] Nicéan barks of yore—ships that sailed from the ancient town of Nicéa long ago.
[3] o'er—over.

On desperate seas long wont[4] to roam,
      Thy hyacinth[5] hair, thy classic face,
Thy Naiad airs[6] have brought me home
      To the glory that was Greece,
And the grandeur that was Rome.[7]

Lo! in yon brilliant window-niche[8]
      How statue-like I see thee[9] stand,
      The agate[10] lamp within thy hand!
Ah, Psyche,[11] from the regions which
      Are Holy-Land!

---

[4] wont—accustomed; used to.

[5] hyacinth—like a sweet-smelling flower.

[6] Naiad airs—fairylike tunes.

[7] In these two famous lines, Poe celebrates the ancient days of classical Greece and Rome.

[8] in yon brilliant window-niche—in the brightly lit, window opening over there.

[9] thee—you.

[10] agate—made from marble or quartz.

[11] Psyche—goddess of the soul.

The Raven

"The Raven" (1845) gave Poe his first major success as a writer. Poe's purpose for writing this poem was simple. He wanted to show his readers a mind filled with "fantastic terrors."

Once upon a midnight dreary, while I pondered,
    weak and weary,
Over many a quaint and curious volume of
    forgotten **lore**[1]—
While I nodded, nearly napping, suddenly there
    came a tapping,
As of some one gently rapping, rapping at my
    chamber door.

---

[1] **lore**—facts, stories, beliefs.

"'Tis some visitor," I muttered, "tapping at my
    chamber door—
        Only this and nothing more."

Ah, distinctly I remember it was in the bleak
    December,
And each separate dying ember wrought its ghost[2]
    upon the floor.
Eagerly I wished the morrow[3]—vainly I had
    sought to borrow
From my books surcease[4] of sorrow—sorrow for
    the lost Lenore—
For the rare and radiant maiden whom the angels
    name Lenore—
        Nameless *here* for evermore.

---

[2] dying ember wrought its ghost—smoldering logs in the fireplace made
flickering lights.

[3] morrow—morning.

[4] surcease—an end to.

And the silken, sad, uncertain rustling of each
purple curtain
Thrilled me—filled me with fantastic terrors never
felt before;
So that now, to still the beating of my heart, I
stood repeating
"'Tis some visitor **entreating**[5] entrance at my
chamber door—
Some late visitor entreating entrance at my
chamber door;—
This it is and nothing more."

Presently my soul grew stronger; hesitating then
no longer,
"Sir," said I, "or Madam, truly your forgiveness I
implore;[6]
But the fact is I was napping, and so gently you
came rapping,
And so faintly you came tapping, tapping at my
chamber door,
That I scarce was sure I heard you"—here I
opened wide the door;—
Darkness there, and nothing more.

---

[5] **entreating**—asking for.
[6] **implore**—beg.

Deep into the darkness **peering**,[7] long I stood there
 wondering, fearing,
Doubting, dreaming dreams no mortal ever dared
 to dream before;
But the silence was unbroken, and the stillness
 gave no token,
And the only word there spoken was the
 whispered word, "Lenore!"
This *I* whispered, and an echo murmured back the
 word, "Lenore!"
  Merely this, and nothing more.

Back into the chamber turning, all my soul within
 me burning,
Soon I heard again a tapping somewhat louder
 than before.
"Surely," said I, "surely that is something at my
 window lattice;
Let me see, then, what thereat is,[8] and this mystery
 explore—
Let my heart be still a moment and this mystery
 explore;—
  'Tis the wind, and nothing more!"

[7] **peering**—looking carefully.
[8] thereat is—is there.

Open here I flung the shutter, when, with many a
flirt and flutter,
In there stepped a stately raven of the saintly days
of yore;
Not the least obeisance[9] made he, not an instant
stopped or stayed he;
But, with mien[10] of lord or lady, perched above my
chamber door—
Perched upon a bust of Pallas[11] just above my
chamber door—
Perched, and sat, and nothing more.

Then this ebony bird **beguiling**[12] my sad fancy
into smiling,
By the grave and stern decorum of the
countenance[13] it wore,
"Though thy crest be shorn and shaven, thou," I
said, "art sure no craven,[14]

---

[9] obeisance—bow or curtsy.

[10] mien—the appearance.

[11] bust of Pallas—statue of Pallas Athena, the Greek goddess of wisdom.

[12] **beguiling**—deceiving.

[13] countenance—face.

[14] craven—coward.

Ghastly grim and ancient raven wandering from
   the Nightly shore—
Tell me what thy lordly name is on the Night's
   Plutonian[15] shore!"
            Quoth the raven, "Nevermore."

Much I marvelled[16] this ungainly fowl to hear
   discourse so plainly,
Though its answer little meaning—little
   relevancy[17] bore;
For we cannot help agreeing that no living human
   being
Ever yet was blessed with seeing bird above his
   chamber door—
Bird or beast upon the sculptured bust above his
   chamber door,
            With such name as "Nevermore."

---

[15] Plutonian—of Pluto or the lower world; hellish.
[16] marvelled—was amazed.
[17] relevancy—relationship to the matter at hand.

But the raven, sitting lonely on the **placid**[18] bust,
    spoke only
That one word, as if his soul in that one word he
    did outpour.
Nothing farther then he uttered—not a feather
    then he fluttered—
Till I scarcely more than muttered, "Other friends
    have flown before—
On the morrow *he* will leave me, as my hopes
    have flown before."
               Then the bird said, "Nevermore."

Startled at the stillness broken by reply so aptly
    spoken,
"Doubtless," said I, "what it utters is its only stock
    and store,
Caught from some unhappy master whom
    unmerciful Disaster
Followed fast and followed faster—till his songs
    one **burden**[19] bore—
Till the dirges of his Hope that melancholy burden
    bore—
               Of 'Never—Nevermore!'"

---

[18] **placid**—calm.
[19] **burden**—chorus or refrain.

But the Raven still beguiling all my sad soul into
  smiling,
Straight I wheeled a cushioned seat in front of
  bird, and bust and door;
Then, upon the velvet sinking, I betook[20] myself to
  linking
Fancy unto fancy, thinking what this **ominous**[21]
  bird of yore—
What this grim, ungainly, **ghastly, gaunt**,[22] and
  ominous bird of yore
      Meant in croaking "Nevermore."

This I sat engaged in guessing, but no syllable
  expressing
To the fowl whose fiery eyes now burned into my
  bosom's core;
This and more I sat divining,[23] with my head at
  ease reclining
On the cushion's velvet lining that the lamp-light
  gloated o'er,[24]
But whose velvet violet lining with the lamp-light
  gloating o'er
      She shall press, ah, nevermore!

---

[20] betook—started.

[21] **ominous**—fateful.

[22] **ghastly, gaunt**—shockingly thin.

[23] divining—discovering.

[24] gloated o'er—saw with spiteful admiration.

Then, methought,[25] the air grew denser, perfumed from an unseen censer[26]

Swung by Seraphim[27] whose foot-falls tinkled on the tufted floor.

"Wretch," I cried, "thy God hath lent thee—by these angels he hath sent thee

Respite[28]—respite and nepenthe[29] from the memories of Lenore!

Quaff,[30] oh quaff this kind nepenthe and forget this lost Lenore!"

> **Quoth**[31] the Raven, "Nevermore."

"Prophet!" said I, "thing of evil!—prophet still, if bird or devil!—

Whether Tempter sent, or whether tempest[32] tossed thee here ashore,

Desolate, yet all undaunted, on this desert land enchanted—

---

[25] methought—I thought.

[26] censer—jar or bowl for burning incense.

[27] Seraphim—angels.

[28] **Respite**—rest, relief.

[29] nepenthe—drug used to forget grief or suffering.

[30] **Quaff**—drink deeply.

[31] **Quoth**—said.

[32] tempest—storm.

On this home by Horror haunted,—tell me truly,
     I implore!
Is there—*is* there balm in Gilead?[33]—tell me—tell
     me, I implore!"
               Quoth the Raven, "Nevermore."

"Prophet! " said I, "thing of evil!—prophet still, if
     bird or devil!
By that Heaven that bends above us—by that God
     we both adore—
Tell this soul with sorrow laden if, within the
     distant Aidenn,[34]
It shall clasp a sainted maiden whom the angels
     name Lenore—
Clasp a rare and radiant maiden whom the angels
     name Lenore."
               Quoth the Raven, "Nevermore."

---

[33] balm in Gilead—soothing ointment in Israel; a biblical reference.

[34] Aidenn—Muslim paradise, Eden.

"Be that word our sign of parting, bird or fiend!" I
shrieked, upstarting—
"Get thee back into the tempest and the Night's
Plutonian shore!
Leave no black plume[35] as a token of that lie thy
soul hath spoken!
Leave my loneliness unbroken—quit the bust
above my door!
Take thy beak from out my heart, and take thy
form from off my door!"
Quoth the Raven, "Nevermore."

And the Raven, never flitting, still is sitting, *still* is
sitting
On the pallid bust of Pallas just above my
chamber door;
And his eyes have all the seeming of a demon's
that is dreaming,
And the lamp-light o'er him streaming throws his
shadow on the floor;
And my soul from out that shadow that lies
floating on the floor
Shall be lifted—nevermore!

---

[35] plume—feather.